The Grand Catharsis

Ken Kalb

An AstroLog of the Shifting Ages

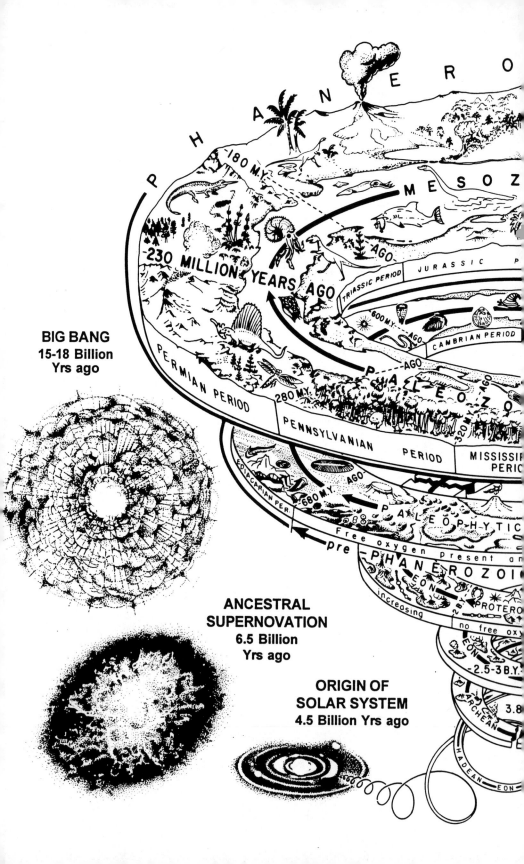

P H A N E R O

MESOZ

-180 MY-

230 MILLION YEARS AGO

TRIASSIC PERIOD | JURASSIC P

AGO

600 MY- AGO

CAMBRIAN PERIOD

PALEO ZO

PERMIAN PERIOD

280 MY

PENNSYLVANIAN PERIOD

MISSISSIP PERIO

EDIACARIAN PER.

680 M.Y. AGO

PALEO-PHYTIC

Free oxygen present an

pre-PHANEROZOI

EON

increasing

2 B.Y. PROTERO

no free oxy

2.5-3 B.Y.

3.8

ARCHEAN

HADEAN EON

BIG BANG
15-18 Billion
Yrs ago

ANCESTRAL
SUPERNOVATION
6.5 Billion
Yrs ago

ORIGIN OF
SOLAR SYSTEM
4.5 Billion Yrs ago

THE TIME SPIRAL
by DAVID CROUCH

The Grand Catharsis
An Astrolog of the Shifting Ages
by Ken Kalb

Published by Lucky Star Research Institute
Box 5796
Santa Barbara, CA 93150

Library of Congress Catalog Card Number 94-78382
ISBN 0-964927-6-9

12345678910

FIRST EDITION—1994

$14.95
This book may be purchased from the publisher. Please add $3.00 for postage.
Phone orders: 1-800-626-2721 ext 405 (charges only) or 1-800-969-4401

 Printed on 100% recycled paper.

Dedication

Like the planets & satellites
who have chosen
orbits around our Sun
This is for those who
are my Circle of Light
and shine in
a Golden shrine
of Immortality
in my Heart....
and for those
future lights
yet to be
discovered

Acknowledgements

Special thanks to: My clients who have supported the Lucky Star Astrological Chart Service over the years who helped make my research and writing possible. The tireless Jeffrey W. San Marchi who has published my articles for many years in his Ojai Valley Voice with courage, accuracy, taste, and excellent graphics. The multitalented Susan Shapiro who provided extra publishing horsepower and expertise when I needed it. And Lalainya Splies who captured my vision and graced this book's cover with her beauty.

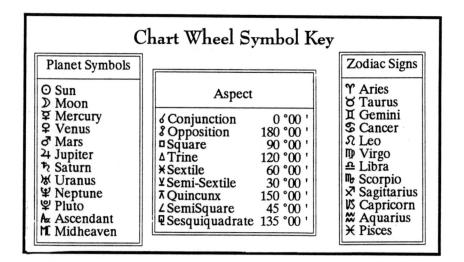

Chart Wheel Symbol Key

Planet Symbols	Aspect		Zodiac Signs
☉ Sun			♈ Aries
☽ Moon	Conjunction	0 °00 '	♉ Taurus
☿ Mercury	☌ Conjunction	0 °00 '	♊ Gemini
♀ Venus	☍ Opposition	180 °00 '	♋ Cancer
♂ Mars	□ Square	90 °00 '	♌ Leo
♃ Jupiter	△ Trine	120 °00 '	♍ Virgo
♄ Saturn	⚹ Sextile	60 °00 '	♎ Libra
♅ Uranus	⚺ Semi-Sextile	30 °00 '	♏ Scorpio
♆ Neptune	⚻ Quincunx	150 °00 '	♐ Sagittarius
♇ Pluto	∠ SemiSquare	45 °00 '	♑ Capricorn
Asc Ascendant	⚼ Sesquiquadrate	135 °00 '	♒ Aquarius
MC Midheaven			♓ Pisces

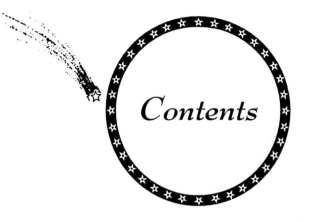

Contents

Weaving Wisdom Out of Time

An Elemental Earth
Soaring through the galactic ooze
A zillion sister ships
accompany her cruise
through eons of laser lullabys
and endless vacuum songs
blending and mixing
surely weaving
a core of mystic lore

A dozen labors to perform
as the Circles spin through Time
A thousand tasks before me
through which I'm gonna shine

Arien flares
Taurean trust
Geminian genius
Cancerian changes
Virgonian virtue
Librean liberty
Scorpionic succulence
Sagittarian sagacity
Aquarian agelessness
Piscean prisms

Weaving wisdom out of Time
The Fires cook as we dine
Dancing to the rhythms of drums and flutes
Golden harps and celestial lutes
A silver chain of mysterious lore
Radiates from deep within our core
An Eagle soars beyond the Sun
On Wings of Silver-tipped
Freedom

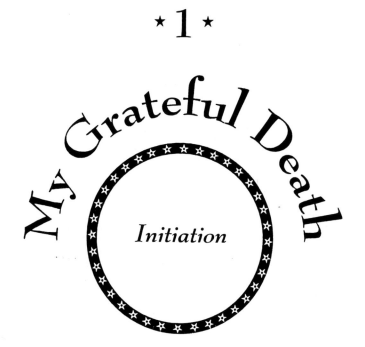

My Grateful Death

Initiation

I was caravaning back after a month of very high adventure from Southern Mexico the night before New Year's Eve in 1968. On the outskirts of Mazatlan, we pulled into a small cantina for food and debate about whether or not to continue North toward home or make camp. I was losing the argument to stay. Kit and Bill were dying to see their girlfriends who expected them at some party, and my partner John was somewhat torn and neutral. My voice of reason tried to explain that we could spend the weekend and experience how this culture brought in the new year, renew our expiring travel cards, and even get some more surf as we made our way casually back home. "But I want to start 1969 in the United States," won out. So we split up with the three of them traveling together in Kit's bug and myself alone in my VW van.

I decided to caravan North with them for a while with the idea of camping at Playa Novillero, about 75 kilometers up the road. I'd been there before and knew it was peaceful and safe, and would likely be serving up some sweet little beach break waves for breakfast. We were rolling over windy hills and dales on a narrow two lane road separated on both sides from the land by barbed wire fencing. It was one of those crystal clear full moon nights with the stars bursting out of the giant sky. I remember I was listening to *Salt of the Earth* from the Stone's new Beggars Banquet 8-track and feeling really good. I began to see a mysterious light over each rise in the hills out in the distance on the roadway; I couldn't tell what it was. My friends were about 200 yards behind me.

As I came over the next rise, suddenly the light was blinding. In a microsecond glance I saw a large cattle truck taking up most of the road, staring me right between the eyes. I couldn't get by him on the right, so with a last ditch survival attempt, I cranked the steering wheel to the left while simultaneously opening my driver's door; performing a James Dean-style *el rollo* out the door and on to the land—letting the van get eaten by the truck.

The next thing I consciously remember was awakening to quite a bizarre scene. Several federales were busy splitting up my possessions; my cameras, clothes, guitar, and money. A wrecker had the back end of my van raised and was rapidly removing the motor. When they noticed I was stirring one of them cried out, *Jesus Christo él no esta muerto!* They had pronounced me dead about a half an hour before, and had commanded Kit, Bill, and John to leave.

Which seemed like eternity to me. I don't even recall hearing the impact. I just remember the full Moon getting closer and closer until I had fully fused with this dimension before gliding beyond. Then I remember soaring through space cradled in divine grace as I expanded into the planets and stars. I felt blissful, peaceful, and fully joyous. I had no fear as I floated freely in this interstellar dimension feeling like I had merged with a greater consciousness which was welcoming, loving, nurturing, caring, and all knowing. Infused with golden-silver light, surrounded by swirling silence in timelessness, I felt like I was being guided somewhere, though my destination was unknown. There was no differentiation between the cosmos and my psyche; they had been engaged and married as though each fiber of my being was connected to a different star. One thing which left an indelible impression on me was the complete interconnectedness of all of the energy in the universe. Another was how vibrantly alive the figures of the constellations of the zodiac were, and how thoroughly intertwined I felt with their energy. The imprint of a vision was forged in my soul which I will share with you throughout my writings.

Then I remember soaring through space cradled in divine grace as I expanded into the planets and stars. I felt blissful, peaceful, and fully joyous.

A heavier flash of density pulsed through my being which carried a question and required a decision. It seemed to ask whether to continue to let go or whether to hold on and go back. I recall making the choice to let go, but I began to be pulled back toward Earth, back to my body.

Things started happening very fast. They loaded me in a truck and took me to the Red Cross hopsital in Mazatlan. In the middle of the night they stitched up my knees and dressed my bruises. From their conversation outside the door I could hear they were planning to take me to jail in the morning where I would await a trial about my accident. I decided to escape.

I made it out of the hospital and down to the beach. All I wanted to do was jump in the ocean. I frolicked in the glassy sunrise surf which elevated my mood, then came ashore and fell blissfully asleep tucked away underneath the pier. I was awoken suddenly to gunpoints in my back and face by three federales who led me by foot to the jail.

The jail was was a 25' by 25' room with a large drain hole in the middle. Prisoners would sit on the floor around the perimeter of the room, with the exception of one who was in a narrow solitary confinement cell. He would awaken every now and then, scream out *viva la revolucion*, run to the other side of the cell and bang his head against the cement wall and pass out. Scorpions who like urine, would occasionally peek out of the drain hole in the middle of the room which served as our *bathroom*.

I was seated in lotus posture rising deep in meditation when I felt an itch on my left side underneath my ribs. It was a scorpion who flipped over and got in a little sting, right about the time I knocked him away. It seemed as though the mixture of blood, adrenalin, and scorpion venom was rushing like a hot snake to my head. I jumped up on the bars and started shaking them furiously screaming at the sargeant to *set me free!* As I shook the bars I could see the cement around them crumbling and the bars loosening, just as 5 federales came over and opened the barred gate to release me at gunpoint.

Anda le pues commanded one of the federales. We marched out of the jail and down the street in front. We continued walking up the hill several hundred yards where at the top I saw a large building which was to become my indefinite new home; the Mazatlan State Prison. Now this was heaven compared to the jail. There was an outdoor courtyard in the sunshine and I could hang out there all day, and watch the stars at night. The perimeter of the courtyard was lined with rooms where the inmates would live. Kilo dealers, thieves, rapists, murderers, wife beaters, counterfeiters, and various other outlaws made up the population, though all were very friendly and welcoming to me. I knew most of their names and did their astrology charts. I would spend my days like an iguana in the sun, doing yoga asanas, meditating, cleaning my wounded knees with lemons and salt, playing a guitar, listening to and telling stories, practicing my spanish, and praying to be set free. As the days melted into more days, it was a strange feeling not knowing if I would ever be released.

About three weeks later I was called into an office where to my surprise they had one of my favorite t-shirts and two pairs of my blue jeans. The captain informed me that my case had gone before the magistrate. They had decided that the accident was *no contest*, with neither party at fault, and I would now be free to go. He told me they had found $33 among my possessions, the exact price of the bus ticket they

had purchased for me for the 28 hour ride up to the border at
Tijuana. My Lucky Stars were starting to light up.

The bus ride was endless. We had been driving for about
14 hours when the driver finally made a stop in Hermosillo to
crash out in a little dorm space behind his seat. I had been
fasting for about ten days and was starving. There was a little
cantina where the driver had stopped, and I decided I had to
eat. The only thing on the menu was steak, and though
contrary to all the rules of any of the dietary regimens I knew,
I negotiated a trade for my spare pair of blue jeans and ate it,
and it was really good. Once back on the bus I found a paper
bag and wrote a poem on the back of it to my partner John:

> *If brother John had come with me*
> *Up the coast toward home*
> *He wouldn't be anymore*
> *but molecules*
> *of blood and flesh*
> *pressed and compressed*
> *A friendly memory*
> *of a golden spirit*
> *released and set free*
> *to dance among the stars*
> *and become one*
> *with the essence of all creation*
> *Until we meet again*
> *my friend*

☆ ☆

I made it to Tijauana where I hitchhiked up to Encinitas
to Swami Yogananda's Self Realization Fellowship, which has
one of North County San Diego's premier surf spots right

Paramahansa Yogananda

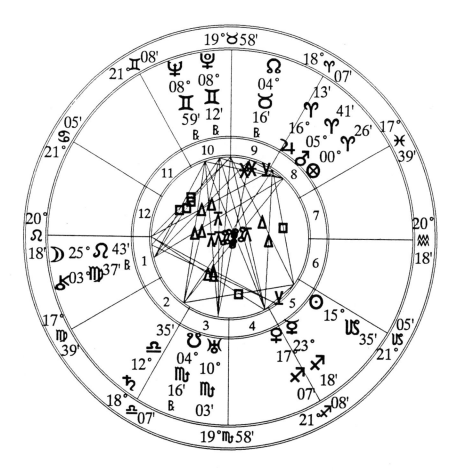

January 5, 1893
8:38 PM
Bombay, India

out in front. It was breaking a clean 3'-5,' and I was able to borrow a board and paddle out. I cannot describe how ecstatic it felt to make the bottom turn on the first wave I rode and continue to carve it up to the end. I was grinning so hard I think I bent my face permanently out of shape. Oh how good it was just to be alive!

After the surf session, I went up to the shrine to meditate. Next to where I was sitting was Yogananda's book, *Authobiography of a Yogi*, the book I had read on the beach in Mexico. I picked it up and casually opened it right to the page which said, "an individual is born at that time and place when the celestial rays are in perfect harmony with his individual karma." I remember thinking that he put that very well.

I returned home to Isla Vista near Santa Barbara, where I worked at Sun and Earth natural foods. It was incredibly heart warming to get bear hugs from friends who had thought I'd passed on, and to realize I was genuinely missed. Though I had lost everything material I had owned, I knew I had gained a treasure chest of riches which I would never lose.

We erected a geodesic dome in the garden of Sun and Earth which was separated into twelve sections, one for each of the signs of the zodiac. A metal sculptor carved out beautiful astrological glyphs, and we planted the herbs and placed the stones and glyphs which corresponded with each of the signs and its ruling planets. In the center was a fire pit surrounded by a hexagon of benches where we would have metaphysical discussions and I could do astrological readings.

So I started my life all over again. Cleansed from my upper middle class background by the death of the accident, I was reborn to the life I came here to live, empowered with a new appreciation for each and every breath of life for which I would be blessed. Sure, I'd been doing the right things—yoga, meditation, music, exercise, diet, social interaction, good deeds—but it took this experience to forge my spiritual committment from 98 to 100 percent. I had undergone my initiation and Grand Catharsis.

That was almost 25 years ago now. I imagine my awakening through death was reflected in the symbology of the Uranus/Pluto conjunction of the 60's. Since then I have filled my time with lots of great adventures and meaningful projects, and have been an active astrologer, metaphysician, and writer throughout.

The following chapters began as an anthology of several of the most requested articles I have written and published over the last twelve years during this awakening period when several waves of consciousness have crested. Each was centered around significant circumstances and key events and issues in our current and future history—interwoven from many perspectives. We need to know where we've come from and how we've grown to gain the empathic understanding of where we're going, what to look for, and how to best tune into it. Much new material has been added to create a mosaic of a past, present, and future chronicling of planetary consciousness, and a guided tour of its amazing unfoldment through a period in Earth history so intensely potent, that I call it the Grand Catharsis.

A few of the articles, like *The Grand Planetary Alignment*, are more astrophysical than astrological in scope, providing clarity & a cornerstone for a grounded understanding of the ominous Earth Change issue. *Astrology Hits the Big Time* provides validation for the science of the stars & disarms the skeptics. *The Prediction Wars* chronicles a critical phenomenon and illuminates fresh views demanding reflections on some important lessons. *Waves of Light and dark* reflects on some phenomenal events in our consciousness journey. *The Stars of Saddam*, penned at the very beginning of the Mid-East crisis centers on a key karmic lynch pin and clearly validates the power of predictive astrology—as does *The Magic 90's* which previews this decade. *The Capricorn Challenge* is critical because the 80's and 90's were so saturated in Saturnian energy and its transformation toward the Aquarian. The *AstroPolitics* series examines America's astrology, political figures, and structures from a deeper, metaphysical point of view to go beyond popular resources. *The Grand Catharsis Formula* captures the flavor of the Uranus/Neptune conjunction and underscores the dynamics of future change. *SuperConjunction 1994* focuses the themes of this period, and is somewhat of a living miracle in astrological prognostication. In one chapter I even take you surfing, not just because it is a love of mine which I'd like to share, but because it provides a centerpiece for the environmental issues we all face, as well as three key attibutes of life; timing, balance, and loving intention. *Great Balls of Cosmic Fire* illuminates a current cataclysm which was also a signature event in our vault in consciousness. The final chapter, *Visions of Aquarius* is almost a book in itself. It gazes into the future and synthesizes all of this material to help create some perspectives on how the *true* new age will all unfold. Each chapter is intended to inspire, remind, teach, refresh, entertain, and hopefully even amaze you with illuminations on both the changes and leaps we are making in our consciousness, and our lives. Whether you are a newcomer or an oldtimer to astrology, I blend and mix in the symbolic sacred science of the stars so you will enjoy and be enriched by the adventure. So come travel with me back and forth through time. We are alive during the most thrilling of times. The following chapters are an interdisciplinary chronicling of key flash points in our current and future history, using creative celestial navigation to take you along with me on a fascinating and meaningful journey through our *Grand Catharsis* into a new millenium and another age.

Ken Kalb
July 11, 1994
Aguada, Puerto Rico

Ain't it good just to be alive
See the stars spinnin' in the sky
See the fire in my lovin' eyes
Ain't it good just to be alive
     —Flaming Arrow

★ 2 ★

The Magic 90's

Originally
Published
January 1990

H appy New Year and Happy New Decade! Goodbye to the eighties; decade of decadence and deception. Hello 1990; Decade of our Destiny. Will we live or will we die, will we laugh or will we cry; will humanity survive itself and create a future? Such ultimate questions are what will be answered during this decade of our destiny.

Number 9, number 9; I hear John Lennon's voice resounding through my skull. Think of it, the mystical magical number 9—the last number before going back to zero. It's the time when all things complete themselves, when we take it to the limit. Three three's in arithmetic, three triangles in geometry; physical, mental, and spiritual perfection in metaphysics. The grand trine in astrology, or the 3, 6, 9 relationship of the ancient Chinese Oracle the *I Ching*, to mention but a few. Then there's *Love Potion #9*, or my favorite place to be, Cloud 9, when everything's going just fine. This is the decade I know I have been preparing for; I am humbled by the honor of being alive! This is the decade for which anyone who now breathes must awaken to the call of our birthright and become part of our creative solution. You, yes *you*—are the hope of the world. This last decade of the last century of what will hopefully not be the last millenium for mankind, is definately our Decade of Destiny. Do you believe in magic?

The vibrational magic infused in the number 9 (and other alchemical shifts we will discuss) gives me hope for the future. We should all allow our own energy to rise from the ashes of the 80's like the mythological phoenix. As the Chinese year of the Snake sheds his skin into this New Year of the Horse on the 27th of January, it's time to get on your favorite pony and ride. Align with what you really and truly care about and take it to a higher octave. Take off your mask, Halloween is over; the game is about to be changed, ladies and gentlemen. Under the 8, the power trip was in vogue where Donald Trump was King, and *he who dies with the most toys wins* was the law of the jungle. But now that the eight of Scorpio has shifted into the 9 of Sagittarius, we must act with vision rather than power, or we simply perish from this magnificent planet. In truth, we must act with powerful vision if we are to survive, and hopefully thrive into the future. Love is service in action, and it's time we get very busy. Indeed, there will continue to be the few who control the many who will attempt to perpetuate the power trips which are destroying the environment, along with all those who are unconsciously helping to execute this destructive program. But some time in this decade this group will be forced to

John Lennon

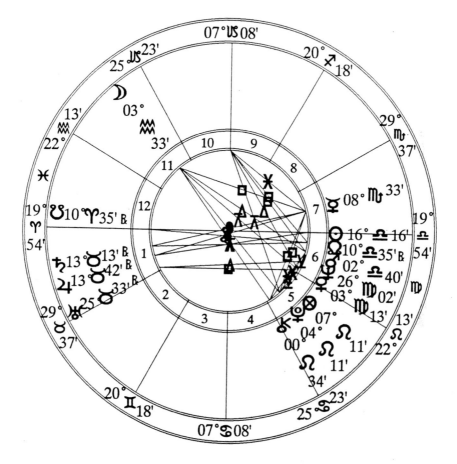

October 9, 1940
6:30 PM
Liverpool, England

22

realize that we are all in this same Earthboat together, where in the face of catastrophe, all humans are brothers and sisters. In the heat of a forest fire, the rubble of an earthquake, the wake of a flood, or the frenzy of economic collapse, there is little difference between black or white, rich or poor, Buddhist or Jew, conservative or liberal, man or woman. We are all children of God in the family of man. The battle lines are now being drawn, because the very destiny of our species, and the well being of the 25,000 other living species on this Earth are all at stake. The evolutionary split will become clearly defined between those who are part of the problem or part of the solution, and each of us will get to choose his path. The linear direction of our civilization, where economic growth is the prime priority is akin to the road runner of cartoon fame darting over the edge of a cliff with his legs furiously pumping in mid-air. Unfortunately this is no cartoon, but it if were, it would be a *loonytoon*, because it's certainly no *merry melody*. I think most people simply want to be happy and live healthy, prosperous, and meaningful lives. But when you consider that *dumb* dinosaurs lasted 100 million years, while *intelligent* humans are struggling with a few thousand, one begins to wonder if we are even capable of survival. You cannot unscramble an egg. But our future is up to us. So we better busy-up here turning things around.

We are all children of God in the family of man.

In the 80's we saw the USA almost become the US of J, with California becoming the East Coast of the Pacific Rim.

Perhaps this is just our Hiroshima karma backing up on us, with the Japanese performing aikido with our desires and greed until we have hocked our soil and our souls. Ah, so. How long will the land of the free and the home of the brave keep buying into this? It might just take an American recession to curb our addictive consumerism, which deflates the Japanese economic balloon. And what about our continuing self-destruction of Mother Earth in the name of progress, or our $3 trillion (and growing) national debt or the Third World's triple-digit inflation rates, greed, overpopulation, hypermaterialism, homelessness, hunger, a.i.d.s, drugs, apartheid, international upheaval, ad nauseum. Just the tip of the iceberg reveals so many iniquities and travesties making so little sense; most of which will be corrected as complex cycles complete themselves: Life will start to resume its dynamic balance simply because failure formulas will run full cycle and crumble, to be replaced by healthy, inspired, ecologically and environmentally balanced alternatives which will begin a rapid growth cycle and catch fire. I forsee powerful new leaders emerging in America who will light the way. The time has come for big change. And despite ourselves, in spite of ourselves, *and* because of ourselves, the changes will come. Our task is to dance through these changes as the heavens and Earth rearrange, in the healthiest and most creative manner possible. Don't you want to dance?

Change is happening ultra-fast as we complete this Piscean cycle and begin the much heralded Aquarian period in the next 6 years. By 1996, when Pluto has finished its long transformational journey through the sign of it's rulership, Scorpio and moves into Sagittarius; and Uranus completes it's 7-year structural revolution in Capricorn and enters the sign of it's rulership in Aquarius, a true New Age will be here. Can you imagine the quantum leaps humanity will make during 7 years of Uranus in Aquarius and 15 years of Pluto in Sagittarius!

But the preceding transitional period will find virtually all structures; personal, social, political, economic, you-name-it, transforming as we figure ourselves out of our many messes and into success strategies, more in tune with our human community in this global village. By welcoming the many changes and rising to the challenges we facilitate this process. Structural transformation is precisely what the current Saturn, Uranus, and Neptune in Capricorn; Pluto in Scorpio phase is all about. We will all get so bent out of our current shapes during this phase, that we will be forced to let go of most of the old ways which got us into this fix, only to create new forms which will custom fit our future.

We will all get so bent out of our current shapes during this phase, that we will be forced to let go of most of the old ways which got us into this fix, only to create new forms which will custom fit our future.

1990-91 will be pivotal as radical events flood the picture. Hard Saturn and Pluto aspects to the USA chart make a karmic war a distinct possibility this year. But popular mobilization for environmental and humanitarian causes will also be strong. Positive, healthy, and ecologically sound alternatives will begin to proliferate the mainstream as the antiquated and greedy destructive structures (like the Cold

Mikhail Gorbachev

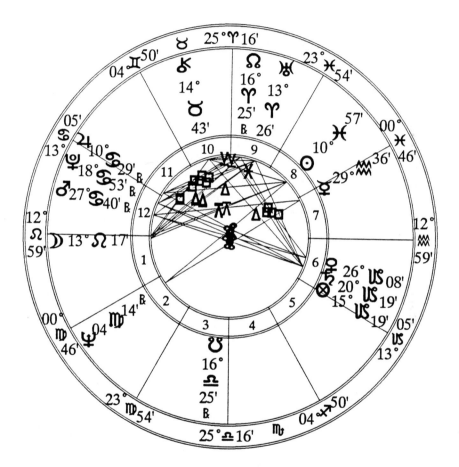

March 2, 1931
2:52 PM
Privol'noje, USSR

26

War) which have been obliterating the environment and economy begin to crumble. Trends toward a healthier lifestyle will continue to accelerate, including higher consciousness toward diet, exercise, holistic medicine, and the war on smoking. Corporate America and Japan will be forced to grow a conscience, and be held accountable for the environmental consequences of their economic activities. Gorbachev's second Saturn return and other challenging transits may find his reign eclipsing and the Soviet Union turning inside out, but he has awakened his people's spirits and set irreversible forces into motion for a positive and possible East European life. Expect our countries and cultures to only get closer. China and the Middle East are the certified wildcards on the international scene, and I fully expect some serious clashes during this decade. On the other hand I also anticipate an end to apartheid in South Africa, with that country actually spearheading new dimensions in human and civil rights. The mid-90's should see new vitality in the economies of the emerging countries in Asia and Latin America, and turnarounds in Europe. Hopefully at some point, wealth will be measured in terms of enhancing life rather than economic growth. But no one should fear the prospect of global economic reorganization if it is necessary to prepare a world for our children, or perpetuates the survival of ourselves and our environment. Wouldn't it be great to live in a world free of debt, where the economy actually made sense? We may just have to start with a clean sheet of paper at some point. Not the end of the world! Wouldn't it be nice to allow our Mother Earth the opportunity to heal her wounds so she may keep rocking her Divine Creation in the cradle of her sweet Love? Let's remember, Father God and Mother Nature are much

Our children coming into
maturity will amaze us with
the magic in their hearts, the
magnificence of their minds,
and the beauty of their
ancient souls: It may simply
be their powerful
Will to Live
which creates our Future

grander and far more ancient than the human ego. They will grace us with the opportunity to make conscious change, but if we don't, their natural cycles will make the changes for us, and we will learn to adapt. Afterall, adaptation is our species strongest suit.

Wouldn't it be nice to allow our Mother Earth the opportunity to heal her wounds so she may keep rocking her Divine Creation in the cradle of her sweet Love?

Isn't it amazing that halfway through this six-year transitional period, Neptune and Uranus, ruler's of the two shifting ages will conjoin in the sky, with the faster moving Uranus lighting the way into Aquarius! This once every 171-year phenomena should begin another cresting wave of consciousness accompanied by a flourishing new Renaissance, where the brilliance of the human spirit will manifest in myriads of magical, yet tangible ways. Early in 1994, the inner planets will conjoin with these two gas giants (Uranus and Neptune), linking the unconscious and the personal in a Capricorn Superconjunction. Many cycles will complete much karma during Saturn's last 2 years in the final sign Pisces, before entering fresh territory in Aries in the Spring of 1996. Angelic Jupiter will conjoin Pluto in late Scorpio at the end of '94 and enter Sagittarius, blessing 1995 with a powerful uplift in its home sign. By 1995, Pluto will also enter Sagittarius after 13 years in the intensely challenging Scopionic dimension. In 1996, Uranus will enter the sign of

Thomas A. Edison

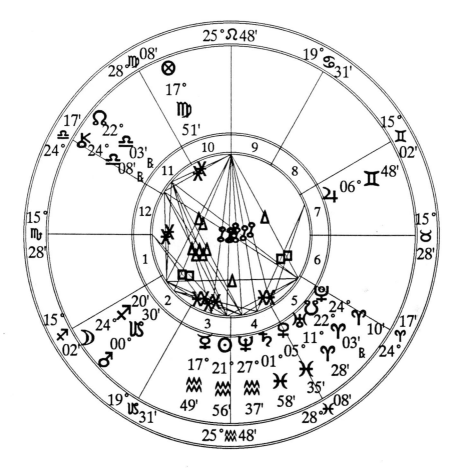

February 11, 1847
6:00 AM
Milan, OH

James Dean

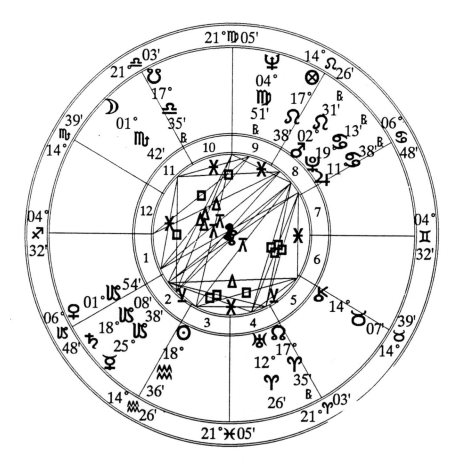

February 8, 1931
2:00 AM
Marion, IN

its rulership, Aquarius, the sign of **magic**. Please mark my words, these planetary shifts will be synchronous with the transition from the Piscean to the Aquarian Age! If you've been searching for the miraculous, by the mid-90's, you may just find it is your life.

Isn't it amazing that halfway through this six-year transitional period, Neptune and Uranus, ruler's of the two shifting ages will conjoin in the sky, with the faster moving Uranus lighting the way into Aquarius!

By the time Jupiter conjoins Uranus in Aquarius in 1997 we will be in a period of magnificent breakthroughs. We will have tapped into clean renewable energy sources, beginning the end of the politics and problems of oil. Wonderful new food sources from the sea, the Sun and the Earth will make living off of questionable cattle obsolete, while world hunger will be diminished. Technological advances will boggle the current mind and be brilliantly applied to all areas of life. Health and medical breakthroughs will diminish human suffering. Political structures will accomodate the freedom of the human spirit. Inspired leaders will emerge who will unite in a vision of love, peace, and cooperation. Nuclear weaponry will become virtually obsolete, allowing scientific development to be focused on raising the quality of life. Our children who are coming into maturity will amaze us with the magic in their hearts, the magnificence of their minds, and the beauty of their ancient souls: It may simply be their powerful will to live which manifests our future. Life, liberty, and the pursuit of happiness will return as top priorities, as the success formula of living our lives in vital balance creates a free, healthy and happy planet.

To be sure there will be powerful birth pangs of this new period. While Aquarius can be the genius, it can also be the outlaw; both Thomas Edison and James Dean were Aquarians. All signs have both their positive and negative polarities. And just as Uranus spins sideways to all the other planets, Aquarius can be the weirdo, the freak; the bizarre and belligerent badboy. Perhaps Jupiter's conjunction to Uranus will also be synchronous with massive social unrest between the haves and have-nots, a new nuclear Napoleonic anti-christ, major Earth changes, or even a President Dan Quayle! But at this moment of the birth of this final decade of the century marching toward the third millenium, I am filled with optimism about the future. I'll elaborate on the Aquarian changeover in much greater detail, including this opposing polarity in the final article entitled *Visions of Aquarius*. Until then, enjoy your magical mystery tour of this decade of deciding human destiny .

I think the magic 90's are going to make the greedy 80's make the wild 60's seem like the sleepy 50's.

Follow your rainbow 'til you find your pot of gold
Follow your dreamboat, take the time to search your soul....
For you will gather no moss on this brand new shining day, yea
—Jimmy Cliff

Dawn

In the golden luminescent mystery of dawn
a Reborn magic carries me on
through and beyond the creation of life
an atomic fusion of the light
awakens the power of our birthright
churns the nectar in our heart
every moment each day we make a new start

Alchemical transformations are spiraling high
with the birth of this day I heave a sigh
in diamond radiance all darkness dies
to the chord of love and life at the center of my self
I am tied

To seek and strive, to be born and to thrive
into the almighty lava of love I dive
and like a zillion bees from a central hive
we spread the nectar of our lives

In the Passionate pounding of the sea
a beckoning call of eternity
bathes each moment in mystery
and from the succulent kiss of ecstasy
erupts the lava orgasm of infinity

✩ ✩

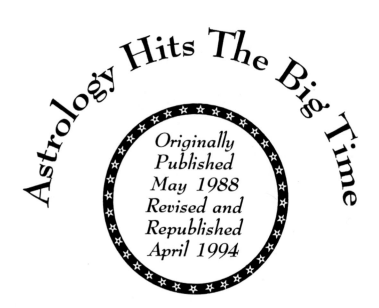

★ 3 ★

Astrology Hits The Big Time

Originally
Published
May 1988
Revised and
Republished
April 1994

I sn't it ironic that a Republican President, *the Great Communicator* Ronald Reagan was the one responsible for elevating the public dialogue about astrology; whether it is true or false, real or unreal. Upon the disclosure that the President regularly used an astrologer for advice and scheduling; Time, People, most major magazines, newspapers, radio and television talk shows were all suddenly buzzing about planet Earth's ancient art of human understanding. Reagan's Chief of Staff Donald Regan claimed that a good percentage of Wall Street brokers consult astrologers. The Gallup Poll found the *majority* of Americans believe there is some validity to astrology. Don't you just love it!

I wish I could have debated William Ruckseyer on ABC's Nightline show of May 5th on Astrology. You see, science

Ronald Wilson Reagan

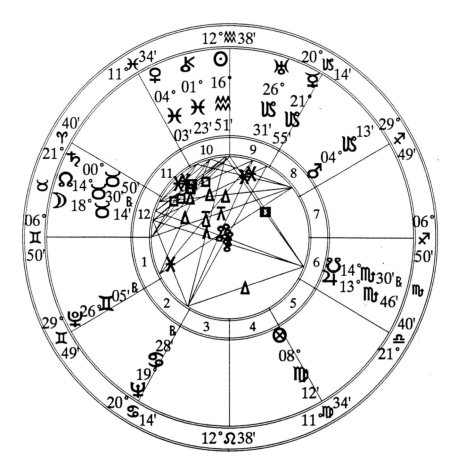

February 6, 1911
06:00 AM (est)
Tampico, IL

does not acknowledge the existence of anything they cannot see, measure, or *prove*. Astrology and other parapsychological fields are *phenomena of consciousness or spirit*, neither of which science has the means to understand, or even identify. I would like to pose the question to Mr. Ruckseyer and his colleagues in the scientific community: *Do you believe in Love?* Well I certainly hope so, because if you don't, there is little hope for us anyway. But if you do indeed believe in love, can you provide some proof of its existence—perhaps measure its specific gravity, hardness, shape, size, or location? I think not! And just because science *cannot* indeed prove the existence of love, does this mean there is none? There's about as much point in talking to *most* scientists about the existence of anything *spiritual* as there is trying to talk a cop out of a bad ticket.

I would like to pose the question to Mr. Ruckseyer and his colleagues in the scientific community: Do you believe in Love?

Until recently. Many in the hard sciences have gone *soft*, as the evolving relationship between the spiritual and empirical merges. Award winning science writer Robert Wright, while describing himself as "a fairly hard-core scientific materialist," adds, "I do like to think there is more to this universe than meets the eye." It is indeed in current scientific vogue to attempt to explain God, love, consciousness and the mysteries of existence and the universe. Nobel prize-winning physicist Leon Lederman's *The God Particle*, takes aim at bridging this gap so heartfully expressed in Stephen Hawking's hope that someday humankind will "truly know the mind of God." Sixty world-class scientists, including 24 Nobel prizewinners teamed up to publish their cosmic thoughts in *Cosmos, Bios, Theos,* with the co-editor, Yale physicist Henry Margenau concluding that "there is only one convincing answer" for the intricate laws that exist in nature: "creation by an omnipotent, ominscient God." Other popular attempts to merge science and spirit such as Fritjof Capra's *The Tao of Physics* acknowledge that scientific attempts to describe essence are embryonic, akin to a baby explaining the rigors of life to his grandfather. Astrologer Tad Mann surmises that, "scientists are beginning to realize that their theories of natural phenomena, their *laws,* and their mathematics are all creations of the mind itself, rather than objective reality." And astrophysicist George Coyne tips the scales toward a balance when he suggests that "scientists don't *need* God for our scientific understanding of the universe," because "we don't pretend to have all the ultimate answers."

Deepak Chopra has fused scientific and spiritual, Eastern and Western thought into a mind/body quantum theory where the qualitites of the physicist's unified field theory is identical to the mind of God. In this view, there is *no* material universe, because scientists have now found that atoms are broken into subatomic particles which are simply variable fluctuations or impulses of energy and information from the raw material or great *void* of the universe. The only differences between things are in the arrangement, quantity, and frequency of this *non-stuff.*

To most scientists, human life simply boils down to a matrix of metabolic processes, just as the universe consists of

Albert Einstein

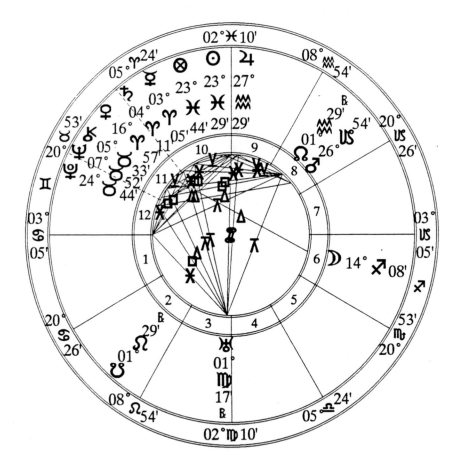

March 14, 1879
10:50 AM
Ulm, GER

the physical structure of space. However, in this material view of life, no more can be learned about the cosmos through external means than can be understood about a human being by examining a corpse. This is really the difference between a living or spiritual view of life and a material or dead frame of reference.

Albert Einstein summarized these disparities quite well when he pointed out that, "the scientists religious feelings take the form of a rapturous amazement at the harmony of natural law which reveals an intelligence of such superiority that compared with it, all the systematic thinking of human minds is seen as an utterly insignificant reflection."

Science has undoubtedly provided a myriad of masterful applications for humanity in a wide variety of areas. But let's remember, modern science *is* only a few hundred years old, and while it certainly has its place, it also has its limitations. Using science to understand the mystical and the sublime is kind of like opening a bottle with a can opener. It's the wrong tool for the right job. Science can certainly quantify God's body, but has alot of difficulty understanding the divine heart and soul. That job is the task of Self realization through human consciousness. It is interesting to reflect on the words of the great British astrologer John Addey when he suggested that "astrology will change science far more than science will ever change astrology."

Now let's stir the pot a bit by putting on our thinking caps. The common factor linking astrology, physics, and psychology is *Time*. Einstein's correlation of energy, matter and time in physics occurred synchronistically with the correlation of psyche and psychology by Freud and Jung. Einstein concluded that the universe was finite, that it must

John Addey

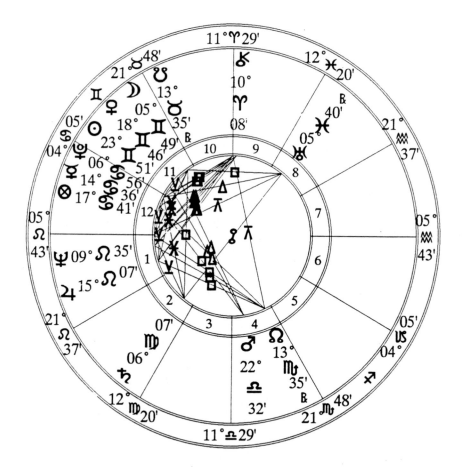

June 15, 1920
8:15 AM
Barnsley, England

have begun with an event and proceed until it terminates in an event. Time is thus circular (see the Time Spiral, page 2), and space and time are a continuum (or perhaps cylindrical like the DNA double helix) wherein every moment from commencement is interconnected to the whole *being* of the Universe. Jung tells us that memories of the entire universe of space and time lie within everyone waiting for discovery because of this interconnectedness, and simply need translation into some form of meaning. Astrology is one language within which time, space, and meaning merge.

When responding to a query of whether or not he believes in astrology, President Reagan gave an astonishingly honest answer: "I don't know enough about it to say if there is something to it or not." I wish all of the closed-minded columnists who have been lambasting astrology were nearly so judicious. As Albert Einstein once quipped, "a wise man's words to a fool seem foolish," so I imagine people in the know will have to remain content to glow in the dark until there is more illumination on the matter.

Having dealt with tons of astrology for many years, I can tell you it is *very* polarizing: People either get it or they don't. You can debate theories of the way the universe works all day and night, but when it comes right down to it, the bottom line on astrology is simply that *it works!* All cosmic speculation aside, the best body of empirical proof I have witnessed on the validity of astrology has been the computerized reports which the **Lucky Star** astrological service has prepared over the last twelve years. The simple fact is that thousands of interpretations have been generated and *everyone* says they fit quite well. Last year we sent out postcards to all of our clients requesting a rating on our

Carl Jung

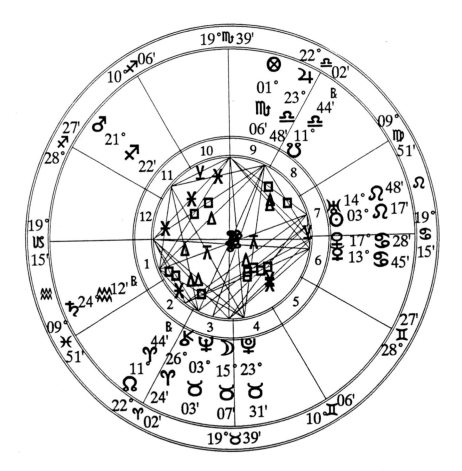

July 26, 1875
6:52:40 PM
Kesswill, Switzerland

The Grand Catharsis

Dane Rudhyar

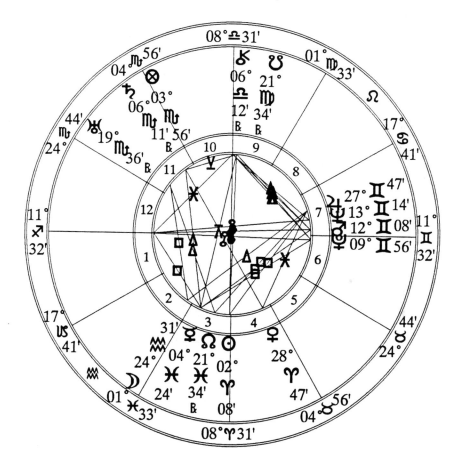

March 23, 1895
12:21 AM
Paris, France

44

astrological reports from one to ten in several categories, and we averaged a 9 on accuracy. And *everyone* answered "yes" to the question "did your report describe you well." So if a team of top astrologers can compile the interpretations to all of the different astrological aspects, components, combinations, and various other factors, and a computer can synthesize and publish them into an analytical report which virtually everyone feels fits them, wouldn't you say there must be *something* to it? This marriage of astrology with computers is also one of the finest examples I've witnessed of the blending of wisdom and knowledge with science for furthering human understanding. And it is in this type of merging where the oneness of truth may be approached.

One of the obvious problems I believe I correctly assume, is that these columnists and other detractors are mistaking the *horoscopes* they read in their newspapers and magazines for genuine astrology. Sunsign astrology, where the population of the planet is divided into twelve character types—or about 400 million people per sign—is at best marginal astrology, and at worst, *pure unadulterated rubbish!* Genuine astrology uses precise and complex mathematical formulae, the latest computer technology, and the intuitive interpretations of highly intelligent individuals with finely trained minds from many years of study and consultation. Another problem astrology suffers is that it is a very complex body of knowledge which takes years of study to master, and special communication skills to deliver. Unfortunately, there is a tremendous amount of astrological amateurism, misconception and misunderstanding flying around which has little to do with professional astrology. Just as you wouldn't allow a hobbyist brain surgeon to work on your medulla

Johannes Kepler

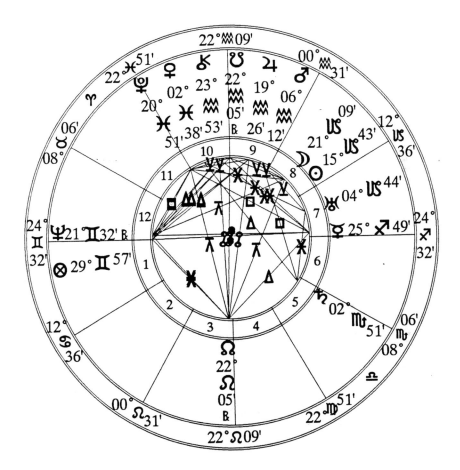

December 27, 1571
2:01:02 PM
Weil der Stadt, Germany

oblongata, it's probably not a good idea to get a half-baked astrology reading. Like virtually anything, it's best to do it right or not at all. On the other hand, a well rounded and grounded professional astrologer can provide powerful tools for self understanding, and navigating your ship of self through the rapids of life.

Astrology is an eleven thousand year old body of knowledge existing *simultaneously* in virtually every culture and civilization on this planet during every historical period right through our present times. History's greatest minds: Plato, Pythagoras, Hippocrates, Aristotle, Ptolemy, Galileo, Copernicus, Newton, Kepler, Lilly, Jung, Rudhyar and so many others have contributed to the generation and refinement of this brilliant technique by which we earthlings can better understand ourselves. How dare some cement-block Washington columnist or other naysayer berate the *divine science*, when he probably knows as little about it as he does of quantum mechanics, or *auto* mechanics for that matter! Sir Isaac Newton summed up the argument on the validity of astrology well when he retorted to Sir Edmund Halley of comet fame, "Sir, *I* have studied the subject, *you* have not."

From the moment humans first gazed at the stars, there has been astrology. Born with no owner's manual other than wealth of internal knowledge resident within our spiritual intelligence, we have probed deeply within our souls and into nature and the universe for the truths of our existence.

☆ ☆

Sir Isaac Newton

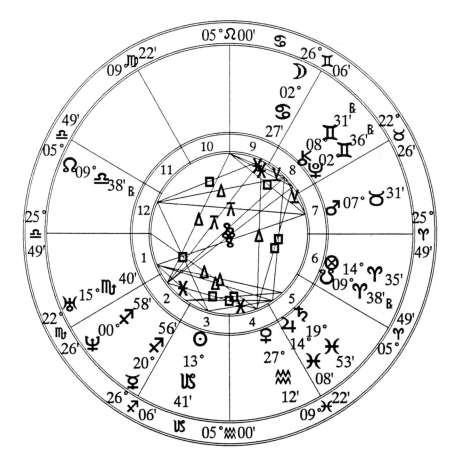

January 4, 1643
1:38:06 AM
Woolsthorpe, England

Adolf Hitler

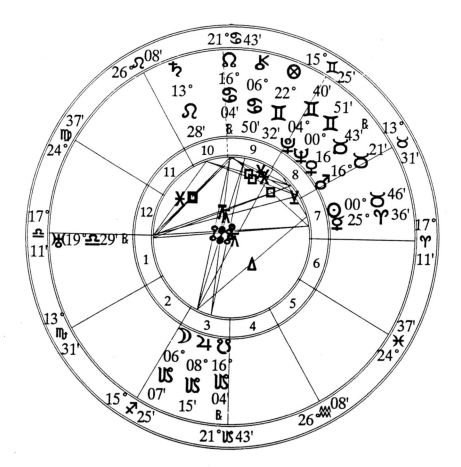

April 20, 1889
5:38 PM
Braunau am Inn, Austria

49

The fact of the matter is that astrology has been widely used by governments for centuries all over this planet. In modern times, Hitler and the Nazi's reportedly planned their strategies astrologically, and FDR and *his* astrologers countered similarly. The Nazi's even engaged in publishing fictitious birthtimes to throw American astrologers off their scent, in some World War II style *Star Wars*. It should come as no surprise that our leaders use astrology. Personally, it makes me feel a lot better that President Reagan did consult this powerful technique for understanding the *moment* and timing events. Why all governments, corporations, businesses, and individuals are *not* using modern astrology is a more plausible question than *why they are.*

My only criticism of the Reagan episode is that much of Ms.Quigley's brand of electional astrology seems a bit cryptic, deterministic, and manipulative. Modern astrology is very positive. It attunes one to swim with, rather than against the tide; to flow with the forces of life and the universe. It is based on the research and analysis of the components of hundreds of thousands of charts. For an individual, a business, or a government to consciously hoist their full sail into the heart of the wind is to operate at full potential; a good success strategy for these challenging times.

From the moment humans first gazed at the stars, there has been astrology. Born with no owner's manual, only the infinite well of internal knowledge resident within our hearts and spiritual intelligence, we have probed deeply within our souls, nature, and the universe for the truths of our existence. Like the Beatle's famous lyrics, "life flows on within you and without you," astrology also says, "as above, so below;" reflections on how existence is an interactive mirror of both

Franklin D. Roosevelt

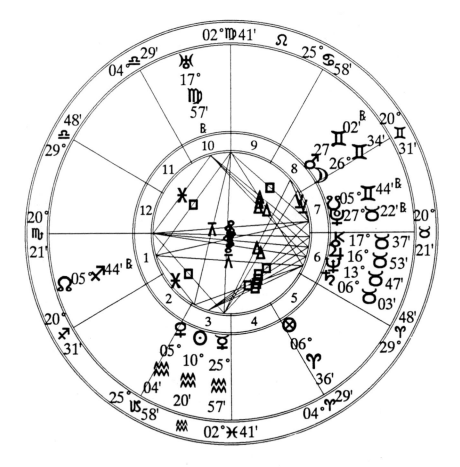

January 30, 1882
1:41 AM
Hyde Park, NY

internal and external realities, synchronistically blending within the *moment*. Astrology is the art and science of the moment; where the past, present, and future may be found. It is a highly scientific and deeply intuitive analysis and understanding of certain moments, each impregnated with a unique energy code; like the DNA of the human cell. By examining the positions, characteristics, and relationships of the unique astrochemistry at the *moment* of a birth or an event, we have learned how to understand and explain the dynamics of personal psychology, history, and the future in a variety of creative, accurate, useful, and valuable ways. In ten thousand years of stargazing, astrologers in virtually every culture and civilization have transmitted this simple realization: There is a mutual synchronicity between the movements of the heavens and our lives here on the Earth. The transmission, evolution, and refinement of this analysis of the intricately woven, yet inseparable relationship between psyche and cosmos has engendered a rich and powerful *new* astrology, to help us better understand who we are and where we are going. This wellspring of archetypal knowledge and our free will to make choices are two of our most valuable human gifts. Let's champion the brilliance and the freedom of the human spirit! ✩ ✩

All truth passes through three stages. First it is ridiculed. Second it is violently opposed. Third it is accepted as being self evident. —Arthur Schoepenhauer

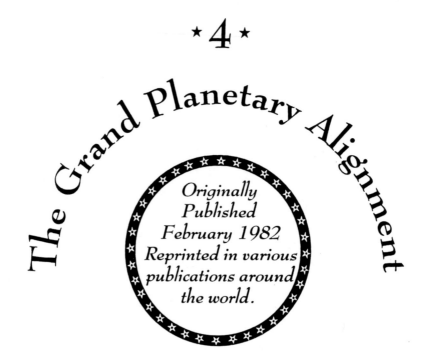

★ 4 ★

The Grand Planetary Alignment

Originally Published February 1982 Reprinted in various publications around the world.

The most severe weather of the century throughout most of the Midwest and South. Torrential rains causing widespread destruction and death in Northern California. Killer Storms in many European countries. The worst border earthquake in 126 years rocking a huge area from Eastern Canada down to Southern Connecticut. A swarm of more than 100 tremors shaking normally stable Arkansas. Strange natural disasters almost daily all over the globe.

Is this nature as usual, or is something extraordinary going on? The beginning of 1982 has indeed been strange and disastrous. But it may be only be a prelude to genuine cataclysms yet to come.

Such was the forecast of a scholarly and well-documented book entitled *The Jupiter Effect*, coauthored in 1974 by Cambridge astrophysicists John Gribbin and Stephen Plagemann. The book targeted 1982 as a time when meteorological and geological activity would build up and become intensely magnified thanks to a variety of physical mechanisms operating simultaneously. Highlighting the forecast was a massive and disastrous earthquake on the southern section of the San Andreas Fault near Los Angeles.

Synthesizing a variety of research projects from the past two decades showing interrelationships of sunspots, solar tides, planetary alignments, disturbed weather patterns and changes in the speed of the Earth's rotation, the authors claimed to have found a trigger capable of rousing regions of geologic instability.

The author's wrote that when the planets in our solar system swing into their rare grand alignment later in 1982, the squeeze will be put on that trigger, and voila: Bye, bye L.A.!

Now before you pack your bags and hock the family farm, bear in mind that the theory has recently been largely debunked. In the June 1980 issue of Omni magazine, Gribbin himself, though still embracing the basic principles of the theory, wrote that he might have gotten the exact year wrong. Dr. K.L. Upton of Griffith Park Observatory feels that the claims do not stand up to scientific scrutiny, and might have even been just a hoax perpetrated to cash in on the lucrative market for sensationalist books.

But despite the doubts of the theory's most drastic detractors. the bizarre coincidence of our savage weather and intensified seismicity this year with the scenario forecast in

The Jupiter Effect cannot be ignored. Planetariums and observatories across the country report that their phone lines have been deluged with inquiries about *The Jupiter Effect*, the grand alignment of the planets, and the scientific prophecy of a doomsday in 1982.

So now that the fateful time is dawning, let's re-examine the theory and its objections, so you may draw your own conclusions on the matter.

"When the planets in our solar system swing into their rare grand alignment later in 1982, the squeeze will be put on that trigger, and voila: Bye, bye L.A.!"

THE THEORY

To fully understand the research and reasoning behind *The Jupiter Effect*, you may wish to read the book, still in print and usually available at your local bookstore. In the meantime, the following is a summary of the book's basic corollaries and conclusions.

Gribbin and Plagemann found a variety of independent research forging a link between solar activity and terrestrial seismicity, particularly during the peak years of the approximate 11-year sunspot cycle. During these peaks, which have remained fairly consistent since Galileo first discovered sunspots in 1610, there are a maximum number of solar disturbances including sunspots, solar flares, solar prominences and coronal holes.

Apparently, these dramatic disturbances of the Sun's equilibrium blast powerful pulses of charged particles through space and into the Earth's ionosphere. This theoretically creates an upsetting effect on the overall circulation of the huge masses of atmospheric weather patterns, which can alter the speed of the Earth's rotation, and thus change the length of our day. In turn, this sudden slowing of the Earth, even by just a few milliseconds, causes extreme stress on the tectonic plate margins where earthquakes occur.

The authors then pointed to a variety of research indicating that alignments of the planets magnify the various forms of solar activity, and in turn bad weather and geological activity on the Earth. They cited the research of Dr. E.K. Bigg of Sydney, Australia which found that the planet Mercury had a magnifying effect on sunspots, most likely due to a tidal influence from gravitational attraction, much like our own Moon creates tides on the Earth. Further research by Dr. Bigg found that this *Mercury Effect* was compounded when one or more of the tidal planets (Venus, Earth, or Jupiter) was on the same side of the Sun as Mercury. Among much additional evidence, Plagemann cited the research of a NASA colleague that found a 20 percent increase in solar activity when Jupiter and Saturn were in conjunction.

"The wealth and variety of coincidence is remarkable, although too often it has either been ignored or kept quiet by the discoverers themselves, afraid perhaps of ridicule," Gribbin and Plagemann wrote.

So when they found that *all* of the planets in our solar system would be clustering in a relatively narrow arc on the same side of the Sun at approximately the same time as the next peak in the sunspot cycle, the case seemed crystal clear.

"From time to time betwen 1982 and 1984 we imagine there will be bursts of strong activity associated with the unusual series of alignments," wrote the Cambridge astrophysicists. "A remarkable chain of evidence, much of it known for decades but never before linked together, points to *1982 as the year in which the San Andreas Fault will be subjected to the most massive earthquake known in the populated regions of Earth in this century.*"

So here were two respected scientists from Cambridge University, one connected with NASA, the other with a prestigious science journal (*Nature*), writing a book with a foreward by the revered Isaac Asimov—making one of the most astounding scientific forecasts of all time!

"A remarkable chain of evidence, much of it known for decades but never before linked together, points to 1982 as the year in which the San Andreas Fault will be subjected to the most massive earthquake known in the populated regions of Earth in this century."

THE PLANETARY ALIGNMENTS OF 1982-1984

A typical diagramatic representation of the solar system would show the nine planets randomly splattered around the 360 degree plane of the Sun. Now, visualize these same concentric orbits, but with all of the planets clustered in a narrow bunch in a small slice of space (see illustration, page 56). During the years 1982-1984 there will indeed be several occasions when all or most of the planets will gather in a series of rather tight groupings.

The actual effects of such planetary alignments, if any, have been a topic of speculation and controversy for many years. Since this phenomenon only recurs every 179 years (according to the authors), modern science lacks much empirical data. Gribbin and Plagemann, however, point to records showing a series of violent earthquakes on the San Andreas Fault in late 1800 that rocked San Juan Batista through Santa Barbara, damaging areas as far south as San Diego. But contending scientists have retorted that these earthquakes preceded the actual *grand alignments* of that period by a few years.

But *The Jupiter Effect* does not pinpoint a precise date for the earthquakes, rather an approximate period that highlights 1982. Nor does it delineate just what combination of planetary alignments and sunspots would actually depress the doomsday device.

Subscribers to the theory logically deduce that the danger dates must be during the closest concentration of planetary alignments. Speculators thus pinpoint March 10 of 1982 when all nine planets will be clumped within a somewhat narrow arc (95 degrees) on the same side of the Sun, forming five approximate planetary conjunctions. Furthermore, massive Jupiter (1300 times the volume of Earth) with its powerful magnetic field will be positioned almost directely at the midpoint of the alignment. To ice the March 10 cake, the Moon will be full, creating a syzygy; another factor which many scientists believe accentuates the occurrence of earthquakes.

Even if we survive the March 10 episode of *The Jupiter Effect* without fanfare, don't sign off on this theory just yet. The next two years hold a host of other propitious planetary positionings, particularly if one planet is removed from the picture. On May 25, for example, all planets except Venus will be grouped within a 64-degree sector, including five approximate planetary conjunctions. The same day in 1983 will find the planets almost as tightly grouped, but with six approximate alignments. Or perhaps April 25 of ominous 1984 will prove unusual, when all of the planets except Mars will cluster within just 60 degrees, with five of them forming a grand conjunction in the constellation of Scorpio.

I am personally looking well ahead to the Capricorn Superconjunction of January 11 1994 as a very drafty "window of vulnerability" for Earth changes, eventhough it occurs slightly after the 1991-2 sunspot peak. But it is the mighty May 4-5, 2000 Grand Alignment right during the peak of the sunspot maximum, with Jupiter at the center of the seven planet Taurean cluster which triggers feelings in my gut of some real busting loose rocking and a rolling.

I am personally looking well ahead to the Capricorn Superconjunction of January 11 1994 as a very drafty window of vulnerability for Earth changes.

Then again, these periods of alignments may just pass us by without rocking our Earth-boat any more than usual. And if there are to be geological cataclysms, my feeling is that God's graceful nature will provide plenty of warnings.

The Big One?

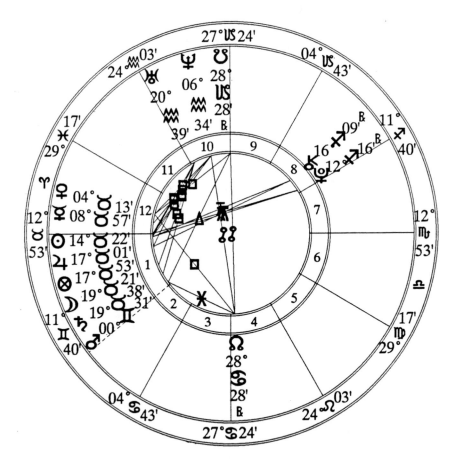

May 4, 2000
6:00 AM
Los Angeles, CA

THE FAT HITS THE FIRE

Such a bold and dramatic forecast could not help but irritate exposed nerves among many spheres of interest. *The Jupiter Effect* has found many adversaries armed with a powerful arsenal of criticism. The majority of scientists feel in fact, that the theory stands in defiance of science.

One of the basic criticisms questions the ability of the planets, no matter how accurately aligned, to exert enough gravitational force to significantly raise solar tides or otherwise accentuate solar activity. Dr. Edward K.L. Upton of Griffith Park Observatory claims that the maximum tidal influence of the Sun is 20,000 times weaker than the corresponding lunar tides on the Earth, and amounts to only 1 millimeter in height. Furthermore, he points out that "the planets beyond Saturn cannot increase the tides by as much as one percent under any conditions." Noted Belgian astronomer Jean Meeus adds that "when it is even suggested that Pluto may contribute to the triggering of sunspots, we may wonder whether the two authors are competent or serious."

But Gribbin and Plagemann insist that the links between planetary alignments and solar activity are both solid and significant. Citing a study by Dr. K.D. Wood of the University of Colorado, they claim that between 1600 and 1972, the dates of (solar) tidal height and sunspot maximum rarely differed from each other by more than a few months. But they also contend that while the planetary effects on solar tides are beyond question, they are likely to be less significant than *other* forces that the planetary resonances exert on the oblate spinning Sun. These magnetic and hydrodynamic forces "affect both the external tidal and the inertial forces within the Sun," and are not fully understood by science. They claim that "as the planets, especially the giants, move around the Sun, they swing it backwards and forward and around, like circling ice skaters holding hands with one another."

Supporting scientists have interpreted these planetary influences which theoretically enhance sunspots, in terms of *electromagnetism* rather than gravity. Sunspots are large centers of intense magnetic force that vary in magnitude from the size of the Earth to that of Jupiter; with hundreds spreading across the face of the Sun at a given time. These scientists speculate that when the planets align on the same side of the Sun, their powerful magnetic fields (particularly Jupiter's) interact with the magnetic fields of the sunspots, and cause them to *grow*. Other scientists think that a preponderance of sunspots can cause a decrease in sunlight by 1 or 2 percent which can also affect weather. On the other side of the coin, astronomy professor Frank Marshak of Santa Barbara City College points out that "both gravitational and electromagnetic forces drop off as the square of the distance." Thus, the vast reaches of space should diminish these forces into insignificance.

Another criticism often leveled at *The Jupiter Effect* has to do with whether the planetary alignments are really all so *grand*. The cover of the book rudely exaggerates the phenomenon, depicting the alignment to resemble pearls on a string, which is indeed a gross misrepresentation of the actual configuration. Astronomer Jean Meeus, writing for the *Astronomical Society of the Pacific*, notes that "the closest all nine planets will ever assemble during this period is within a heliocentric sector of 95 degrees." Though this does represent

An Astronomical Mandala

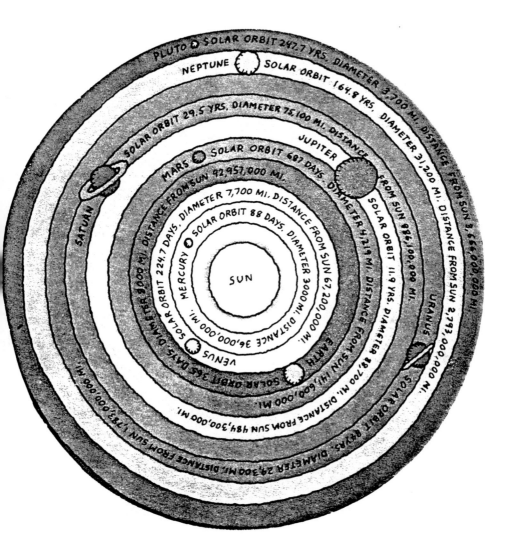

a rather close clustering of the planets, Dr. Meeus asks, "is this an alignment?"

Additional objections have centered around the discrepancy between the dates of the sunspot maximum and of the planetary alignments. The peak of the last sunspot cycle is generally believed to have been in 1980, with the number of sunspots per day averaging around 160 (incidentally, 1980 did experience twice as many *significant* earthquakes as 1979, as well as the fury of Mt. St. Helens). But in his *Omni* article, Gribbin claimed that the entire basis of the theory might be in jeopardy because the sun seemed to be reaching its peak too soon!

A SOLAR SURPRISE

But on this point the plot suddenly thickens. An examination of sunspot activity for the first five weeks of 1982 (see table) indicates that the Sun has been in a veritable frenzy. According to the Solar Forecast Center in Colorado, the average number of sunspots for this period is more than

Table of Observed Sunspots

January					
1	161	13	74	26	190
2	171	14	135	27	182
3	166	16	158	28	264
4	174	17	178	29	287
5	137	18	199	30	289
6	115	19	234	31	398
7	131	20	181	February	
8	182	21	217	1	410
9	173	22	120	2	266
10	141	23	112	3	303
11	69	24	151	4	293
12	75	25	132	5	289

Information: Frank Cowley, Duty Forecaster, Solar Forecast Center, Colorado

180, *with certain days recording 400 observable sunspots!* This raises some interesting questions. Since Gribbin questioned his own faith in *The Jupiter Effect* strictly because he thought the Sun's activity might be declining, wouldn't it now be renewed with the Sun's current vigor, precisely at the time of his original forecast? Hopefully the good doctor will provide some clarification of the matter, unless he's exiled himself in some exotic paradise.

One point on which all scientists agree is that some day in the not-too-distant future the southern section of the San Andreas Fault will slip and cause a disastrous earthquake. The S.A. Fault marks the margin of the Pacific and North American tectonic plates which are slowly but surely separating. The land mass from Baja California to San Francisco is accumulating increasing strain as the underlying plates move North and West by two to three inches a year, while the surface crust remains stationary. This stress has been building up since the fault was relieved by the last major earthquake 125 years ago at Fort Tejon. Scientists concur that the fault is now long overdue for a tremendous slip of about 30 feet, capable of producing an initial eanhquake greater than magnitude 8 on the Richter Scale, or about the same intensity as the Great 1906 San Francisco earthquake, whose initial jolt destroyed over 28,000 buildings.

But it is the mighty May 4-5, 2000 Grand Alignment right during the peak of the sunspot maximum, with Jupiter at the center of the seven planet taurean cluster which triggers feelings in my gut of some real busting loose rocking and a rolling.

HEROES OR HOAXERS?

D**r.** Upton claims that *The Jupiter Effect* is so riddled with flaws and errors that "it is difficult to resist the suspicion that they (Gribbin and Plagemann) do know better, and that *The Jupiter Effect* is a gigantic deception." He complains that "in *The Jupiter Effect* we find an amazingly uncritical acceptance of whatever supports the theory and a total obliviousness to any data that would underimine it." Upton is simply puzzled how two bona fide members of the scientific establishment could exercise such a pseudoscientific treatment of evidence. He suggests that the answer may be found in the book's continual focus on California, where "one finds a fear of earthquakes combined with a proven market for sensational books." In the very same January, 1982 issue of the *Griffith Observer*, in which Upton called the theory a hoax, Gribbin wrote, "it is too early to be complacent, and solar activity needs to be watched for another year or so after maximum before the Jupiter Effect link can be forgotten (this time around)." This award winning scientist and author of several books sticks by his guns, still toying with his *trigger theory* for a cataclysmic doomsday in 1982!

This award winning scientist and author of several books sticks by his guns, still toying with his trigger theory for a cataclysmic doomsday in 1982!

Perhaps the truth dwells somewhere between the polemics of the designers and detractors of the theory. There are literally hundreds of solid research studies linking planetary alignments and solar activity with stimulated terrestrial weather and geological activity. But why are these authors focusing so strongly on the Big One in L.A., and not on earth changes in Columbia, Bolivia, Japan or Indonesia? I think they're both on to something *and* pulling something off simultaneously. In India, millions of people are planning to be focused in meditation and prayer on March 10th in reaction to this prediction. From California, thousands of people have scattered to relocate and start up in new digs. Unfortunately, human lives are being powerfully impacted from the fear generated by this prediction, which seems to be quite possibly motivated or at least exaggerated by greed. And if this fear formula proves to be a real cash cow, how many more times will it be milked before the turn of the century? Please beware! But if there is indeed some truth to the connection between solar activity and earth changes, will this baby go down the tubes with all the dirty bath water? I certainly hope not, because the acid truth of the matter may be valuable.

But if Californians do suffer the monster earthquake this year, Drs. Gribbin and Plagemann will likely be celebrated as prophets. If not, *The Jupiter Effect* will probably fade away with all the other suspicious predictions certain Southern Californians seem so vulnerable to. But even if March 10 goes by without a wiggle or a wobble, we have the future years to watch, and some clues to check out and piece together. Hurricanes, floods, tornadoes, volcanic eruptions, and earthquakes are all part of nature's way, challenges humans have survived for centuries. I see *ourselves* as a far more perilous threat to our own survival. But while I like to stay keenly aware, I also do not like to act from fear. There is a delicate line between awareness and paranoia in the human psyche. So I'll just keep following the Sun and the planets and my own inner feelings for messages and guidance as to when the thin skin of this planet's surface will wrinkle once again. And until then, I'll be singing zip-ah-dee-dooh-dah, zip-ah-dee-ay; my oh my what a wonderful day!

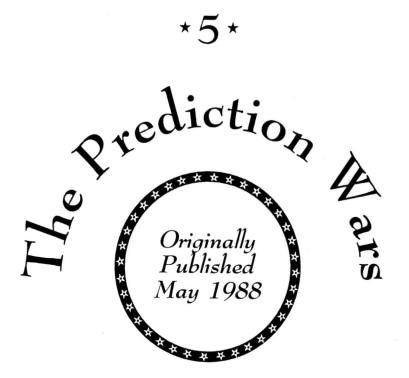

★ 5 ★

The Prediction Wars

Originally Published May 1988

In the last two months I've been deluged with a floodtide of inquiries concerning the possibility of the *Big One* coming to Southern California in May of 1988, as psychic astrologer Michel de Nostradame, *the man who saw through time,* supposedly prophesied back in the mid-sixteenth century. I even found it necessary to leave the following message on the *Lucky Star* answering machine, echoing the words of the late great Meher Baba; "Don't Worry, Be Happy: *There will be no big quake in L.A. in May!*" Indeed, Southern California will most likely experience some massive earthquakes between now and the next twenty years; the former probably being closer to the mark. Just as scientific studies show how cats and dogs and birds and bees flee prior to earthquakes, attuned humans should get early warning

Meher Baba

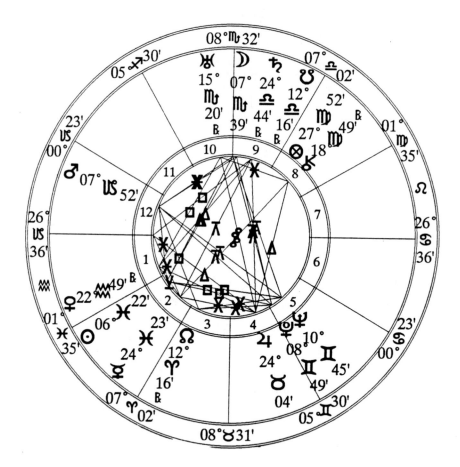

February 25, 1894
4:35 AM
Bombay, India

signals. But the Nostradamus quatrains don't move me a bit, and the scads and slathers of psychic predictions which are likely using the Nostradamian information as their substantive basis are truly a cartoon; and a loony tune, cause they're certainly no merry melody. Here's why:

First, how egocentric Southern Californian's are when it comes to earthquakes. Of the myriads of overdue faults, the *San Andreas* has always proven the most lucrative for those greedy enough to capitalize on the vulnerability of gullible Californians. I am shocked at how virtually *all* the psychics, astrologers, and channels in the area have jumped on this May bandwagon; its like a psychic plague of prediction wars! Ok, I have a proposition for any of you in this professional prediction business: *I am hereby willing to bet anyone, right here and now, anything—that it doesn't happen!* Just give me a call; feel free to call collect if you're money is in the same location as your mouth. But if Los Angeles doesn't get the *Big One* in May, I think every trance channel, astrologer, psychic or other oracle who *predicted* this (particularly for May 15th at 3 pm) should never be listened to again; particularly if they charged you money to spoon you up this BS. Good people's lives are being impacted; families are splitting up, people are selling everything they own, abandoning their lives, and moving out of fear in reaction to these predictions. And dubious predictions serve only to discredit and dilute the potency of credible prognostications.

Chicken Little's sky has finally fallen. And this is most unfortunate, because Nostradamus has some valuable information about the future, but not for May of 1988. Quite possibly for May of 2000, but we'll be discussing this in more detail later.

Earthshaking fire of the center of the Earth
Shall cause trembling around the new city;
Two great rocks will war for a long time,
Then Arethusa shall make the new river red.' (1:87)

Garden of the World near the new city,
In the way of the hollowed-out mountains,
Shall be seized and plunged into a vat,
Forced to drink sulphurous poisoned waters. (IX:83)

Sun twenty of Taurus, very powerful earthquake
The great theater, will be ruined,
The air, sky, and earth obscured and troubled
Then unbelievers cry out to God and saints. (IX:83)

The trembling so strong in the month of May
Saturn, Capricorn, Jupiter, Mercury in Taurus;
Venus also Cancer, Mars in Nonnay,
Hail larger than an egg will fall. (X:67)

Even if you assemble all of the quatrains to attempt to prove the case for May of 1988, the Nostradamian astrology doesn't work. By the time Venus goes into Cancer, Mercury will have transited far into Gemini. When Mercury is in Taurus, Venus is in Gemini. Close, but no cigar. Furthermore, all of the French scholars I've consulted seem to think *Nonnay* should translate as a Nun (as in a convent) pointing to the sign Virgo, not Aquarius or Pisces where Mars will be. Sure you could say heck, it was a long time ago and the quatrain is fairly close (and afterall he *was* French), but to me that's like being a *little bit pregnant*; there's just no

Michele de Nostradame

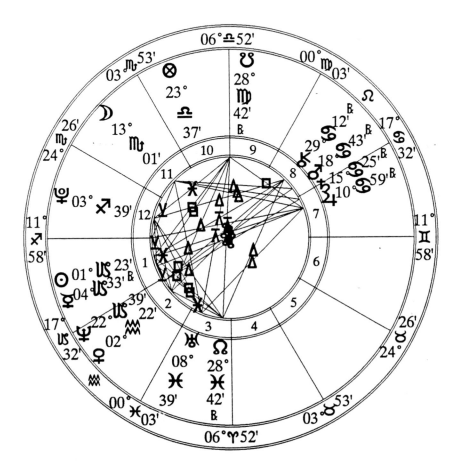

December 14, 1503
6:00 AM
St. Remy, France

such animal! My computer scans have found that in May of 1929, indeed Saturn was in Capricorn while Jupiter and Mercury were in Taurus. But Venus was in Aries and Mars was in Cancer. But hark earthquake fans, my long range scan has found a date which fits the Nostradamian specifications perfectly! Though please, do not hold your breath, because that day is indeed in May ....of 3755! And that's the year the eggplant is supposed to eat Chicago.

If you detect a bit of cynicism, please understand, this prediction seems to get dragged out of the dungeon every May, and the ensuing insanity really requires some levity or else the situation is very dispiriting.

I have alot of other problems dealing with the Nostradamus information, though I do not deny that he seemed to have nailed several predictions. First of all, he wrote in obscure French riddles which he had to conceal and hide to avoid blasphemy, prosecution, punishment and perhaps execution. His writings had to be found, compiled, translated, interpreted, & then debated about and understood. You see, back in the mid-sixteenth century, popular thought still considered the Earth to be flat, and the actual *center* of the universe. Not merely one planet of many, orbiting around one Sun in our Milky Way galaxy which alone houses some 200 billion other Suns, many of which also have solar systems. This is not to mention the 100 billion or so other galaxys postulated to swirl in the deep reaches of space. When Polish astronomer, Aquarian Nicolas Copernicus published *On the Revolution of the Celestial Spheres*, outlining the heliocentric model of the solar system in 1543, it was against strong protests from the church & state. Kepler, Tycho Brahe, and Gailileo & only a handful of others embraced

You are Here!

OUR PLACE IN THE GALAXY

Our Sun is one of 200 billion stars banded together by gravity in an enormous spiral disk called the Milky Way Galaxy. The arrow shows our position more than half way out from the center. It takes light a 100,000 years to traverse our Galaxy, one of billions of galaxies in the universe. Yet all light is ever present in the timelessness of our hearts and souls.

the theory and rejected the Aristotelian and Ptolemaic models, and it took almost 100 years to be accepted—they even sentenced Galileo to life imprisonment for heresy for expounding the new cosmology. So back when the Pope was the religious leader of our very finite and definite center of the universe, astronomers and astrologers had to be very careful with exposing their modern views of time and space. The *man who saw through time* did not want to be hung from his quatrains, so he shrouded them in mystery and obscurity.

In my 1982 *Grand Planetary Alignment* article, I pointed to January of 1994, and particularly *May of 2000* as possible ripe periods for earth change activity because of strong planetary lineups, which is possibly the time Nostradamus was visualizing. In future articles I'll keep you abreast of my research and thoughts on this, though for now I think we'll just have to await the reincarnation of Chicken Little's sky.

THE PREDICTION WARS HEAT UP

Michel de Nostradame and Edgar Cayce are like the E.F. Hutton's of the psychic world; when they talk, people listen. Strong past track records validate speculations on their future visions. The problem is they are *not* talking because they are not with us, and their prophecies from the past are being revived by spirits whose intentions are not always pure.

It was much worse *last* May. J.Z. Knight who channels *Ramtha* gathered thousands of followers in various venues at exhorbitant rates to tell them that Los Angeles would experience a devastating 9.6 earthquake creating such profound earth changes as to kill hundreds of thousands of

Edgar Cayce

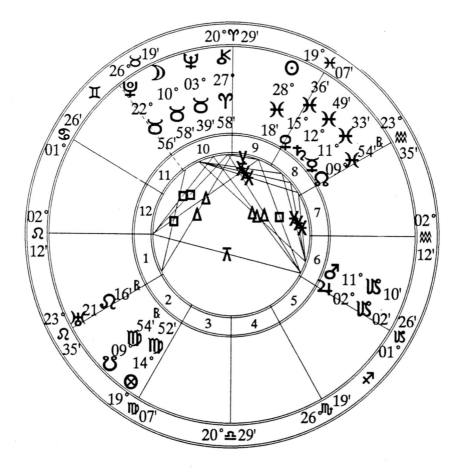

March 18, 1877
1:30 PM (approx)
Virginia Beach, Virginia

humans. People scattered like dust in the wind. My aunt sold her house and moved lock, stock, and barrel up to the top of California. Not to be outdone, Penny Torres who channels *Mafu*, predicted a 9.8 earthquake for a slightly different date, again to various audiences at numerous sites for lots of money. One of my best friends who is usually pretty level-headed, sold his home and moved with his wife and animals up to central Oregon from Santa Barbara. Hundreds, perhaps thousands of people relocated on the basis of these predictions. This proved to be big business, magnetizing tremendous interest so followers would flock to channelings where they would be given clues for their survival and the accompanying spiritual lessons. There was a cash register at every crazy twist and turn on this insanity highway, with the channels raking in big bucks on tapes, seminars, tours, courses, discourses, trainings, and advanced symposiums. One client of mine told me they spent and donated over a million dollars to their channel! But the cake was taken when the quake turned out to be a fake. *So Mafu took the offensive, explaining to his followers that he had gone into the core of the Earth and made some adjustments to relieve pressures to disarm the quake, because mankind was not quite ready for the shift.* Indeed Master.

And people swallowed it up!

But the cake was taken when the quake turned out to be a fake.

57 CHANNELS WITH NOTHING ON

Right now there are so many channels out there you really need a satellite dish or a cosmic cable. I even dated a lovely woman recently who seemed a bit overly inquisitive about my metaphysical perspectives and astrological prognostications. I later found out she was a channel herself when I was played a tape of her beaming in Merlin, Saint Germaine, Commander Romanya of the Pleides, Ashtar, Mother Mary, among others, with the information sure sounding like one of our dinnertime chats—except in strange accents. In Los Angeles, I watched lines form at a *Whole Life Expo* for an individual who would channel a variety of alien space beings, one after another for 3 solid days, telling each what their true mission on Earth was, while accumulating piles of cash. Now I am not negating the existence of the etheric realms or the fourth or higher dimensions from which light beings and information can be channeled. But there is such a promiscuity to this entire channeling phenomenon getting so out of hand right now that it's starting to remind me of that Springsteen song; *"57 channels with nothing on...."* I can only find solace in the affirmation that eventually *only the truth will prevail.* The Great L.A. Earthquake has been predicted so many times I could almost vomit. I can't wait for this channeling fad to blow away in the wind. And this is all very unfortunate, not only for the difficulties it has created for people, but also because there are many of us who are trying to do genuine and sober research in obtaining insights into the mechanisms and timing of Earth changes.

NOSTRADAMUS MEETS CHICKEN LITTLE

The past is really only good for only one thing; to learn from. So perhaps at least there were some vauable lessons which may be found in this exercise. While this current prophet of doom wave will surely crash, I have a feeling others will drag the Nostradamus quatrains out of the dungeon again, particularly as we approach the Third Millenium. So here's some food for your thoughts.

1. If you want to live in Southern California or other earthquake vulnerable areas, learn to live with and be prepared for earthquakes. If not, perhaps the May 1988 fiasco has helped you decide where you really want to be and who you truly want to be with.

2. Your intuition is your highest council. So follow your heart, believe in yourself, and trust your judgement. Our intuition is our truest guide and the choices we make from within are the best one's possible because they are our own.

3. Beware of spiritual teachers who are sensationalist, seem paranoid, or charge excessive amounts of money. Money *is* the law of the economic jungle, but check your oracle's *balance* before you invest.

Earthquakes preceded us by four billion years, will continue after we're extinct, and do not threaten the survival of mankind on Earth. Most certainly no one wants to be in a major earthquake. But we should be more concerned with such

Jimi Hendrix

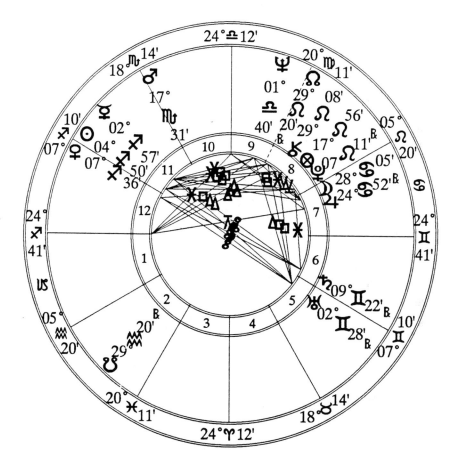

November 27, 1942
10:15 AM
Seattle, WA

matters as not destroying our environment, the quality of our character, our health and well-being, and our goodwill to our fellow humans, than in the inevitability of natural phenomenon or the proliferation of fear. In the words of my childhood guru, Sheriff John, I suggest we try to *"laugh and be happy!"*

And the Wind Cries............Mary
—Jimmy Hendrix

Waves of Light and Dark

A Medley of
Excerpts from the
Lucky Star Gazette
1988-1991

Reflections on a Successful Harmonic Convergence

Fall 1987

The fact that literally millions of people participated in this summer's *harmonic convergence* is convincing testimony that a strong ray of hope illuminates the uncertain destiny of mankind. It is truly awesome that so many people mobilized to sacred sites, geomantic power points, and special places within, simply on the basis of a faith in the theory that human consciousness can transform the course of our history. If we indeed have the power to change our own lives, we must collectively be able to affect social and political change. And for anyone who didn't participate on August 16 and 17, 1987 there's good news: Those dates simply marked the very beginning—the dawn of a reactivation period of the christ or light spirit, so its not too late to climb aboard the peace train.

No the Earth didn't shake, the *space brother's* didn't materialize, nor did anything resembling a feathered serpent pop out of a tree and declare himself the new benefic planetary hero. Myths are internal archetypes, and I've always interpreted the rebirth of Quezoacotl to be the reawakening of the christ spirit or light body within each of us. So when Jose Arguelles speaks of a certain number of people necessary to create a *phase shift*, he means there needs to be enough inertia to ignite a chain reaction of this spirit to connect up a true network of light on the power meridians of this planet. Strong light medicine! It will take consistent faith and teamwork to perpetuate this process. But I consider the phenomenon to be a major success as it crested a subtle vibrational wave of light which will raise the entire planet's consciousness to a sweeter and braver octave—note by note— from now on. No, everything will not be just *ducky* henceforth; usually the brighter the light shines, the darker the shadow becomes; and admist this illumination there will be massive transformation and strong elimination. Afterall, we are all on the wild Pluto in Scorpio ride through 1995. Things will probably be getting better and much worse simultaneously; but ultimately better. It makes me think of the Native American's tribal spirit of unity, or the wagon trains which settled the American West; and how no one would have made it alone. Teamwork, group endeavor, and cooperation are some of the ingredients of the success formula we will have to adopt in order to survive. It is therefore

Harmonic Convergence

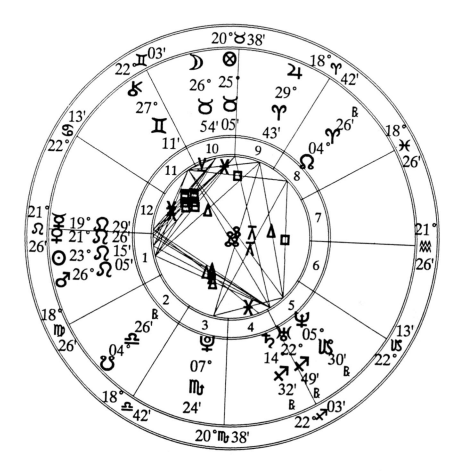

Aug 16, 1987
06:00 AM
Haleakala, Maui

penultimately critical that we carry this spirit forward into concrete, moment to moment action in the weeks, months, and years ahead. Perhaps the harmonic of light set forth by this summer's convergence spirit has already permeated the mass unconscious with new radiance as signaled by the freshly proposed nuclear disarmament treaty or the Pope's peace odyssey. With all of the inner planets aligning in Leo during the event, millions of hearts were merged and linked in warmth, love, and light. And for all the cynics, like those who referred to this event as the *harmonica convention*, you missed some very jamming melodies which may well just keep the entire dance prancing into the future.

THE SATURN/URANUS CONJUNCTIONS

January 1988

Uranus entered Sagitarrius on November 17th of 1981 and Saturn entered on the same day in 1985. In the next six months (Fall 1987-Spring, 1988), these giants of vastly differing character will race toward the first of 3 rendezvous at the molten lava point of the zodiac—where the lightning hot tip of the Sagittarian flame begins to take earthly molten lava form in Capricornian tangibility. Then during all of 1988 they will continue to rock back and forth and play tug of war within a few degrees of each other in late Sag and early Capricorn. The conjunction on February 12, will come back again in retrograde motion on June 26 and directly on October 18. What a conspicuous conjunction to initiate the year of the double eight. Uranus represents the new; awakening, change, brilliance, sudden events, innovation, and revolution. Saturn, almost conversely, symbolizes the old; structure, government, tests, lessons, and limitations in its more rigid realm. This point of their conjunction, at the tip of the archer's lofty arrow magnifies this shift. For not only is this point right on the world axis *and* cardinal winter solstice meridian, but it is also closely aligned with the very *heart center* of our galaxy! This conjunction is happening right on one of the most powerful *cusps* in the zodiacal belt; the zone between the last and first degrees of a solstice point. Furthermore, the first and last degrees of any sign are its most powerful. The first because of the initiatory thrust and shift of a new beginning and cycle of energy. The last because the sign is making its final synthesized and focalized expression, releasing or climaxing the energy of the thirty degree cycle of all its degrees. So what is going on is an intense struggle between the old and the new, suppression and freedom, power and the people. Saturn conjuncts Uranus only once every 45 years and rarely, if ever at this point. Neptune has now moved into the early degrees of Capricorn. And the first of the three conjunctions is also activated by a Mars conjunction on this power point. So we have the ingredients for a truly rare and unique set of planetary dynamics—a genuine turning point in human consciousness. This promises to be a year of shifts and reevaluation, a time when we all wring out the towels of our lives, find new solutions to old problems, and new directions and dimensions to direct our energy. You may actually jump planes of consciousness, leave an old cycle behind, and make some new committments. By the end of the three conjunctions, weak links on all levels will snap as you, your friends, the society, and world shifts its orientation. On the global level, structures which are on shaky ground will probably come tumbling down toward the course of least resistance. The Berlin Wall which will face its Saturn return in 1989, and the Soviet Union are prime targets for transformation. With Pluto in the background in transformational Scorpio, the Uranian urge for the freedom of the human spirit will be ignited and intensified, with many structures not able to withstand this force dissolving and reforming to accomodate this growth. I wouldn't doubt if much of the map gets redrawn in the next several years. So the rules are about to be changed on planet Earth. *The Grand Puppeteer* is about to shuffle the cards after he heats them up and cuts the deck. Present social establishments may not be prepared for the change. Our favorite concepts might just be blocking the wave of a karmic floodtide, hundreds of years building up. Flashes of light are beaming through the darkness. Stay centered on your path my dear friends, as we plunge into the auspicious year of the double eight.

THE CANCER CAPRICORN TOTAL ECLIPSES

Fall 1991

Wow, what a Summer! Six planets retrograde, two lunar eclipses, the *most powerful Total Solar Eclipse* in several hundred years: Bizarre weather, geological and political upheavals, lots and lots of changes. Did you redefine what was truly important to you while Venus was retrograde, even if you had to let go or struggle with a certain relationship? Were you going *ten thousand RPM in neutral* during August's *Mercury retrograde*, only to realize you forgot to put it in gear?

The Amount of Time the Planets are Retrograde

If your summer wasn't a bit peculiar, I'd be very surprised. But the good news is that by the time you read this, Mercury (August 31) and Venus (September 13) will have both gone direct, and Uranus (September 19), Neptune (September 26), and finally Saturn (October 5) will also go direct. So the entire solar system will be pick up speed and start rolling full steam ahead through the zodiac. So the fall should mark the start of a *strong new cycle of growth in your life.*

Though I had the opportunity to witness the *total eclipse* on the *path of totality* in Hawaii, my intuition held me back (a blessing because I wouldn't have witnessed it at all because of the cloud cover!) to settle for seeing it *partially* through some welding goggles on a horse ranch in the upper Ojai Valley. But what struck me the most about the eclipse was less the incredible visual spectacle, than the way *time* seemed to *freeze:*

Baba Ram Dass

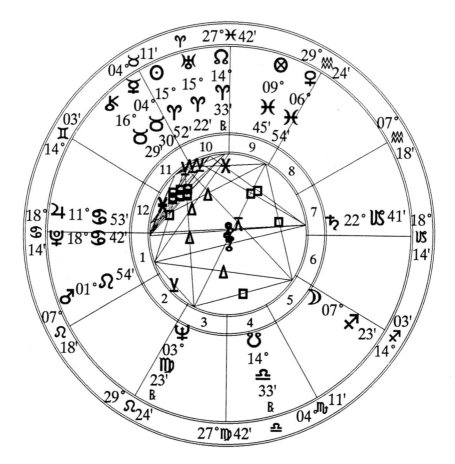

April 6, 1931
10:40 AM
Boston, MA

All of the animals on the ranch were motionless as though posed in yoga asanas, and the feeling within myself was one of an *inner stillness* and peace which I will never *ever* forget. It seemed as though the entire heirarchy of the universe were singing Ram Dass' words, *Be Here Now!*

The zodiacal degree where the Sun and Moon eclipsed was 18' 59" of *Cancer*, and the Cancer/Capricorn axis and all of the issues relating to Mother and Father, on the many levels they can manifest should come storming out of storage right onto your breakfast table. And there will also be another total solar eclipse on this very same axis on June 30, 1992!

The same 19th degree of Cancer is the point where Uranus and Neptune are already flirting with the beginning of the second of the *most significant planetary conjunctions of the Century*. The first being the *Uranus/Pluto Conjunction* of the radical and transformative 60's, activating the tail of the wild Scorpion, creating a tidal wave of *global awakening* in consciousness and a *revolutionary transformation whose shockwave continues to change the world*. As beautiful as was all the peace and love of the period, many people forget that the dark side of Pluto was also awakened and amplified during the 60's; symbolized by the Manson murders or the Altamont debacle. This next conjunction heralds a period of cultural change and an awakening of spiritual values upon which individuals, communities, societies, and nations will reconstruct their social systems more in harmony with the creative spirit of everyone aboard this delicate Earthboat, traveling together through *very* tricky waters. But it will also be accompanied by bright light on our illusions and delusions as well, as Uranus can also illuminate and amplify Neptune's sleazy or escapist side. *I* fully expect to be part of a renaissance period where *new waves of brilliant vision* crest on our horizon, replacing a stodgy old order whose failure formula will peak out, run full circle, to finally be recycled. It is usually when we are at our worst when it brings out our best, and the human condition is ripening for the turnaround. But be patient, because Saturn is in Uranus' sign Aquarius, and Uranus is in Saturn's sign Capricorn; a case of a *mutual reception* of slow Saturnian energy, where the old and the new will wrestle it out for years. And this old Capricornian activity will resonate for 5 more years until Uranus enters Aquarius in 1996. And with Pluto in the Scorpionic background, this process will be complex and wild, and take us to the limit, and perhaps a bit beyond.

Cancer is the sign of the Mother; of creation itself, of nurturing & caring; it's better late than never, but it is definately *time* we accelerate our caring and concern about ourselves and each other; about our community and our planet. I think that deep within the universal unconscious these Capricorn/Cancer eclipses are stopping time for a moment, and calling out to humanity to be more nourishing and maternal, *and* more paternally protective of each other and our planet. And perhaps the signature of this eclipse during this election year in America will be to awaken the feminine principle enough in people who will in turn, elect leaders who *do* truly *care* about people *and* this sweet Earth. In those divine moments of eclipsed inner stillness, I humble myself in awe of the very *miracle of creation*, & devote myself to honoring & nurturing the *lifeforce* & all that perpetuates it.

Our religion seems foolish to you....But so does yours to me.   —Sitting Bull

★ 7 ★

The Capricorn Challenge

Originally
Published
January 1989

The Mountain Goat scales the slopes, head pointed proudly skyward, Christlight vision blazing through his eyes. His feet planted firmly earthbound, at times he springs, at others he stalls; perching to know his path is in sharp focus every single step of the Way. Persevering onward he locks his will on the heights toward which his Vision draws.

Saturn, the Father; sometimes not so sweet Lord of Karma has returned home after 29 years to its own domain in this 10th zodiacal sign, to remind us that the *force* of our actions creates our reality structure, and....our fate. Time once again to face the music, to be held accountable, yes fully responsible; to refine our lives and our world through the eye of karma's needle so we may function more efficiently and in proper alignment with the true needs of our times. For we can be no greater; no bigger no smaller, no better nor worse, no smarter or more stupid, than we just simply are. The time has come to be real and true; to be truly you, which is freedom.

Saturn the *taskmaster* is back in Capricorn demanding a revised vision (or re-vision) and realigned purpose, followed by an ambitious mobilization of our finest energy: Disciplined, consolidated, restrained, committed and dedicated, with well-ordered priorities, for the serious and methodical execution of a carefully refined plan. And let us remember not to forget, everything *is* part of a Divine Plan.

Saturn the *teacher* has returned to the sign it rules empowering us to chisel the structure, form and substance of our lives, our communities, our societies, our nations, and our planet so we may perhaps survive, and hopefully thrive into the future, which at present is looking more and more like a vanishing prospect. But if we are going to reach into the third Millennium, our present course needs drastic correction, right about **NOW!**

Strive to understand this cardinal Earth sign, because the next seven years will indeed be the *Capricorn Challenge*. Saturn will pass through this Seagoat sign for the next two and a half years, Uranus for the next 7, Neptune for the next 9. We will also experience a swarm of solar and lunar eclipses on the Cancer/Capricorn axis, as well as a Capricorn SuperConjunction in 1994; this realm of the Mother and Father, giving birth to new creation on many levels. You, your friends and family, your world and our Earth will emerge from this period like a moth through chrysalis, an Aquarian butterfly. Are you ready for the most radical transformation in planetary history?

Bhaghwan Shree Rajneesh

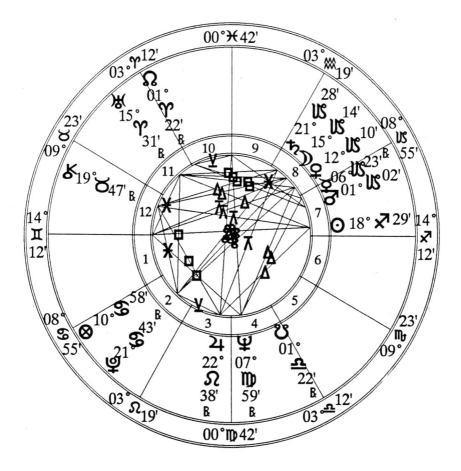

December 11, 1931
5:13 PM
Gadawara, India

We come to this Earth to learn to live in balance amidst once vast resources. One of man, *the toolmakers,* fundamental human attributes is the constructive use of material resources; the ability to civilize. Unfortunately, many humans in their greed have lost sight of this, and are powerfully engaged in an unbridled and indiscriminate scramble for wealth, power, and acquisition, at the unacceptable expense of the quality of life; to the point where we are now quite ominously threatening our very own extinction! Modern man, a mere 10,000 year old newcomer on this four billion year old planet, is well on his way to destroying this jewel in space and the other 25,000 species who inhabit it (including such distinguished 50 million year residents as the dolphins, those incarnations of divine joy)! This must stop at once! Or is it simply *homo sapiens* dubious destiny to quickly flash in Earth's pan and quickly perish? We have yet to prove our ability to survive, and the graffiti is blazing on the wall in glowing neon, warning us to do whatever it takes to get ourselves back in balance. Just because many *powerful* humans have lost the perspective that material things are merely tools, tests, and toys—a means to an end—the tail is wagging our Earthdog silly.

Strive to understand this cardinal Earth sign, because the next seven years will indeed be the Capricorn Challenge.

Perhaps we're in a Rajneeshian-style exercise where we *bop til we drop;* learning lessons by doing things in such excess and abundance that we burn out the desire; like his ownership of 93 Rolls Royce's. For all his spiritual radiance and wisdom, the Eastern Guru, who in this lifetime was born with 5 Capricorn planets, many lessons in material balance were his to learn. I wonder how *Osho* will respond to his Saturn return next year when he faces his multiple *Capricorn Challenge*.

But there is also hope that with this year's Saturn/Neptune conjunction, that we will seize opportunities to reverse this trend and rekindle our *architect's vision* of a viable future for our beloved children. For Saturn in Capricorn can also be the *Master Craftsman in his finest hour*. Solar Capricorn's Martin Luther King and Paramahansa Yogananda are testimony to the power of manifesting inspired vision into concrete form.

Are you ready for the most radical transformation in planetary history?

On the personal level, this year should be a time when things concretize and materialize, feel more solid, committed, stable, and steady in your life. Last year, with the triple Sagittarian conjunction of Saturn and Uranus, it was a period of unpredictability, when many new possibilities were explored, and some genuine breakthroughs made. 1989 should be a year when these new foundations are ambitiously pursued with steady growth and success. That's the good news. But what about our sweet sacred Mother, *Earth*!

Saturn in Capricorn: Karma's mirror. What do we see reflected in our failures in material balance. Dying oceans, poisoned air, ozone depletion, starving multitudes, unlivable cities, greenhouse effect, endangered species, natural imbalances, homeless humans, drug insanity, plagues like a.i.d.s, ad nauseam! Saturn, the ruler of Capricorn has returned to empower us to consolidate the growth we have experimented with and expanded in the last 30 years. Much of this growth has been beyond the threshold of our true needs, pushing the envelope of what may be healthfully and sanely integrated into our world. That is precisely the purpose of the Saturnian cycle; to redefine, cleanse, and challenge the limits and the laws of our new dimensions. Just thirty years ago we launched our very first satellites; now we are arming space for war. But one of too many examples of how far removed from its roots our government has gotten. Thirty years ago fear dictated a policy which has led to a hundredfold increase in planetary weaponry. Today, only communication and love can dismantle this ludicrous arsenal. Fortunately, one Mikhail Gorbachev is on the scene. But it has really only been in the last thirty years that our social, economic, environmental, and political situation has fully gone *berserk*! Will we realize our follies and remember ourselves and the sanctity and balance of Life in time? Not unless we make some radical reversals and commit to being responsible revolutionaries on a mission to create a future!

Saturn demands the highest refinement of personal integrity, and submits us to rigorous tests so we may sacrifice and surrender to be more successful at being the miraculous creatures we are capable of being. Isn't this mystically ringed giant beautiful indeed? But sometimes this is a painful process, though pain *is* the fuel of human evolution. No pain, no gain, eh?

99

Richard M. Nixon

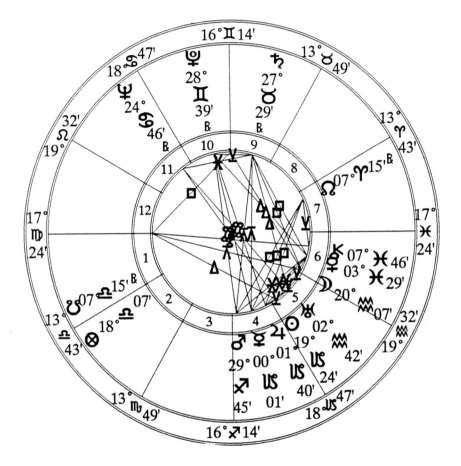

January 9, 1913
9:35 PM
Fullerton Township, CA

From the *moment* humans first gazed at stars until the American Revolution, the boundary between the known and named universe and the unknown—the conscious solar system—was Saturn. It is thus the 'limit' or *gateway* between the conscious and unconscious realms. Saturn in Capricorn teaches us that it is only with our feet firmly planted on the ground and our vision in sharp focus that our minds and spirits may soar in the heavens with purpose, clarity, and meaning. Observe how that which does not prove its true worth to life is blown away by the winds of change. We have entered a period of the selective extinction of that which doesn't serve the future's well-being, accompanied by a rise of all that does. But, knowing the slow but sure nature of Saturn and Capricorn, this will all happen a bit slower than we may like.

Though it is a lot more refreshing to address the higher potentials of the Capricorn phase where it can manifest as the true World Server and even Savior, duality designates a flip side to the Capricorn coin. Archetypically represented by both the Mountain or Sea Goat *and* the Crocodile; this lower polarity is a crafty amphibian who spends a good deal of his time lurking in the mud as swamp king. The lower nature can master manipulation, deceit, betrayal, greed, and disguise to pull off its purely selfish designs. Remember both Benjamin Franklin *and* Richard Nixon were Capricorns.

So what about George Bush and the 41st presidency? Mr. Bush is certainly a competent administrator and a dedicated public servant, though the question marks surrounding his complicity in the Iran/Contra/Drugs/Arms mess are very scary. But the office of the Presidency has miraculous transformative powers. Its occupants often catch fire with a sense of destiny and history-shaping which empowers them to transcend themselves as they rise to challenges and consider their position in history. My feeling is that Bush will soon shed his Reagan-cloned rhetoric and agenda and emerge with very different policies than he voiced during his campaign. One example is our arming for the last thirty years against the Soviet threat in the nuclear Cold War; an expensive and dangerous obsolete fantasy battle. Bush knows that we must now join hands with the Soviets and the other super and secondary powers and focus on the true threats to world peace from certain Arab nations in the Middle East. Though disarmament is simply a practical economic matter (Saturn), he will probably even try to give himself credit for ending the cold war. But at least that means we can go ahead and start trashing the 50,000 or so nuclear warheads we've amassed and concentrate instead on how to most effectively kick some terrorist buttocks. Can we possibly afford a $310 billion military budget amidst the menagerie of our drastic social, economic, and environmental difficulties? The time has come to elevate our consciousness and our world from the destructive depths of fear into the creative glory of love, combining our collective talents as a global community. We surely have all the potential and resources to build a radiant and wonderful future. And I wish George Bush were the enlightened leader detached from the powerful ties to special interests we so desperately need at this time. But short of a sudden Pleidean walk-in, good luck! I expect this Geminian to be a one term foreign policy president whose political future will fail because he does not face the *Capricorn Challenge*.

During Saturn's two and a half year transit through this cardinal Earth sign Capricorn, in perhaps the most intense period in human and Earth history, we will be deluged with a multiplicity of challenges with no simple solutions. And with revolutionary Uranus also in Capricorn for the next 7 years, visionary Neptune in Capricorn for the next 9, and transformational Pluto transiting its own sign Scorpio: Expect structures to drastically transform as you, your friends, our society, our nation, and planet, mobilize to furiously figure our way out of our karmic quagmires, and create a viable future. And with Uranus passing Neptune on its way into Aquarius, this entire process of change will accelerate up to warp speed.

So the game must change, ladies and gentlemen. Man must reverse his current course or we collide with catastrophe. Present social, economic and political establishments must respond to this change. Our very survival as a species is the price we will pay. We may very well be too late, I'm sad to have to say. Do you really think George Bush, greed-driven corporate America, Japan, the Saudi's, or the other power brokers will respond with the inspired radical and visionary solutions we need to get back on track? The stellium of giants in Capricorn notwithstanding, do not hold your breath! So I call on everyone who reads these words to respond. Make whatever life and lifestyle adjustments that will assist your personal and our planetary healing. Use the internal and external resources at your disposal; get serious, focused, be bold and beautiful. But get busy promoting a healthier and happier life. Fortunately, many people have indeed designed lives filled with projects and activities which *are* creating a better world. And God has blessed every human being with the capacity for total transformation at any moment. The light grows ever brighter! For it is truly in our own personal refinement, creativity, and community spirit where we control our destiny, and where our real hopes reside. The rest is in the hands of God.

Perhaps it may just have to be that during this cleansing period our failures will be what engender our success. There may just have to be fires, earthquakes, floods, and cataclysms to bring us together spiritually; an economic collapse to grant an environmental reprieve; or an exhaustion of fossil fuels to clear the air we breathe for life. It would certainly be 'kinder and gentler' if we responded to challenges with action rather than react to emergencies from desperation? So this is the *Capricorn Challenge*: With the brilliance of our minds, the radiance of our spirit, the beauty in our hearts, and the will to live a brighter vision, we must build real bridges into the future. So lets hang in there and keep the radiance of faith burning eternally. It won't be any ideological 'thousand points of light,' but millions of real beings in the light who will illuminate the way. It seems like the future will be a real battle between the dark and light, doesn't it? This bulging planet will be improving and deteriorating simultaneously. But by the time Saturn transits through Capricorn to Aries, Jupiter through Sagittarius and into Aquarius, Uranus moves into Aquarius, and Pluto into Sagittarius; the Millennium will be near and the true Aquarian period here. It is always darkest before the dawn, and we must continue to glow brightly in the dark as this true new age pangs into birth.

Resolution resides one step beyond despair
—Flaming Arrow

Silent Devotion

Containing my Love for you, Sweet Lord
I am compelled to sing
My heart must have a voice
Yet I long to keep the Silence intact
To protect the Temple of this deep Devotion
From the vibrational clutter of random words
Sounds seeking to find what in the sound of Your voice
Can only be found in Silence.......Love Itself
I go deeper within....

Pulsating with the rhythms of the Universe
River of Life, coursing through my body, my world
The Universe unfolds inside me and all around me
Your touch is felt.......Eternal Moment....
The Soul, infused with Light, Eternal Being
Breathes through my pores...the sound of the Wind is heard...

In the Chambers of my Heart
An even greater Light shines, self sustaining
I turn my eyes gently upward, the Light of my Heart follows
As the Mother touches the feet of the Father, Love intensifies
Electric, radiant, pulsating energy turns to sound
Oh glorious thunder of Om....So glorious song of the Soul
The Mother gazes into the eyes of the Father
And they are One. Transcendence
Eye to Eye...Essence to Essence...Light, sound, spirit conjoin
The Word of words is spoken. A Sun is Born!
A Fusion of Heaven and Earth, inflused with the holiest of holy,
Spirit...Realized in the Absolute Presence within each of Us...
The Same

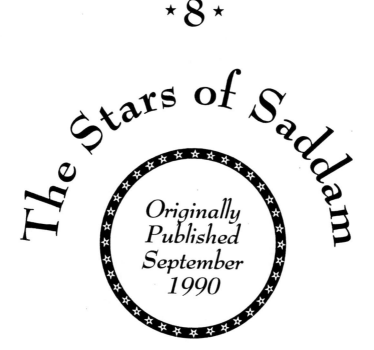

★ 8 ★

The Stars of Saddam

Originally Published September 1990

In the region where modern civilization so humbly began three thousand years ago, the most powerful political, military, and economic forces on planet Earth are jockeying positions and poising for showdown. On the table sit many of the karmic consequences of these three thousand years of *progress*. The voices in the wind sing Nostradamus quatrains, biblical prophesies, psychic predictions, gloomy economic forecasts, and visions of a world very different from the one we now know. At the center of this cyclone is Iraq, a small Islamic country with just half the population of California, yet arguably the fourth strongest military power in the world, and its President Saddam Hussein, a madman who fights dirty.

Saddam Hussein was born with revolutionary Uranus conjunct his Taurus Sun at the Midheaven, forming volatile *hard* aspects to Mars conjoining his fiery Sagittarian Moon. Also throbbing out of his chart is an intense T-square in the active cardinal signs, highlighting expansive Jupiter which sits in perfect opposition to his deathstar Pluto. These are all the ingredients for a methodical, explosive, and unpredictable megalomaniac whose track record includes gassing civilians and losing a million men in an 8-year stalemate with Iran. While the ultra-wealthy oil sheiks of Saudi Arabia sipped champagne and munched caviar on their yachts in the French Riviera, Saddam used his oil resources to amass a devastating arsenal of weaponry and build an army one million strong, strategically located in Planet Earth's most dangerous danger zone. He's a strange brew; a few parts crazy and creative genius, a few parts devious and destructive fool, with some loose wires dangling here and there—holding a torch to the richest oil fields on the Earth. And the United States and Western friends, so thoroughly addicted to this Earthblood which gives life to machines and makes men rich, greedy, and powerful responds with the most massive military buildup since Vietnam.

Is this heavy or what?

The Silver Lining in the Persian Gulf cloud is that this crisis is the best argument this planet has experienced yet for alternative energy, and a peacetime economy which can survive without a military industrial complex. The longer I live, the more I realize that human nature rarely responds from awareness or foresight, but rather from crisis and catastrophe. But these rules are soon to be changed, my friends.

The Silver Lining in the Persian Gulf cloud is that this crisis is the best argument this planet has experienced yet for alternative energy, and a peacetime economy which can survive without a military industrial complex.

Saddam Hussein was born on April 28th, 1937 in Tikrit, Iraq. Though his birth hour is from a rumor, I'm confident that this rectified chart provides a good basis to analyze and focus on what very well may transpire, by examining the movements of the planets ahead in relation to his chart. This Leo rising birthmap gets well validated by his pride, arrogance, self inflation, charisma, dramatic flare, self-centeredness, militaristic leadership role and conquesting nature—besides the huge pictures of himself he has plastered up all over Bhagdad.

Saddam was orphaned at a young age, and was raised by an uncle on a melon and date farm. He received his formal education in Egypt, and then studied law in Bhagdad. With ties to the revolutionary Batthist Party since his early twenties, Saddam rose through the military ranks to his leadership position by rubbing elbows with terrorists who groomed him for his coup to power.

Saddam blitzkrieged Kuwait on the very day transiting Jupiter crossed his natal Pluto and opposed his Jupiter; the perfect trigger point to start something big, transformational, and potentially deadly. In the weeks that followed, the universe filled Saddam's sails with plenty of gusty wind as expansive Jupiter moved into Leo, trining his Saturn in Aries,

Saddam Hussein

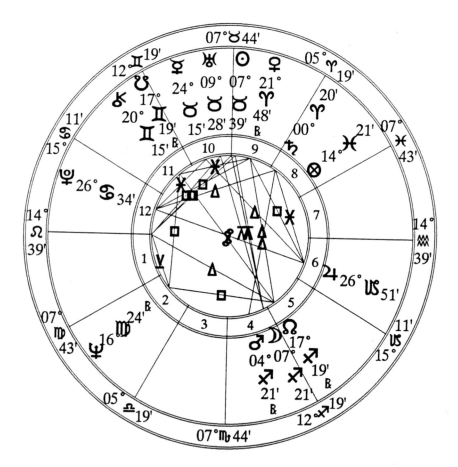

April 28, 1937
12:03 PM
Tikrit, Iraq

as well as his Mars and Moon in Sagittarius. An excellent time for a man of this disposition to charge forth in conquest. With the three outer giants, Saturn, Uranus, and Neptune in the cardinal Earth sign, Capricorn, Mr. Hussein is getting solid support to manifest his will. Uranus in Capricorn is and will continue to trine his natal Sun/Uranus conjunction in Taurus; Saturn is trining his Mercury; Neptune is trining his Neptune; and Pluto is sextiling his Neptune: Translation; in the last two months, Saddam Hussein has become a household word; when Saddam speaks, people listen. He issues a press release that he *may* just go ahead and bomb the Saudi oil fields, and global financial markets lose a hundred billion dollars in a single day! He has *succeeded* in mobilizing the United States and a bit of help from our multi-national friends in bringing the bulk of our conventional weaponry to this complex powderkeg. Around his conquest, brand new alignments and alliances are being forged as the post-Cold War era dawns. And so far, he has tied our hands and feet together as he holds hostages as human shields, points chemical weapons in dangerous directions, and rattles sabres which sizzle the nerves of modern civilization. Thank your Lucky Stars, Saddam, you've been riding your wave of power fairly well. But when will the tide turn?

Among the frightening elements of the Persian Gulf scenario is the apparent willingness of Saddam to take extremely heavy losses, and even go down in flames as long as he can rock the West's already rocky economic boat. Should war break out, his M.O. seems to be to create a meteoric rise in the price of crude oil with the ancillary effect of boosting prices and catalyzing economic chaos. Combined with growing sentiment from heavy Western casualties, plus Arab dissatisfaction with our belligerent presence in their part of the world, Saddam thinks he can send us into retreat.

But with the King of planets, Jupiter, in proud Leo, it will be difficult for either side to back down (though the evolution of Leonion pride *is* humility); a classic clash of wills of two diametrically opposed mentalities. Saddam knows he is sitting in the hot seat of power; a position he may never hold again. For the U.S., the real top priority of the crisis has shifted from saving Kuwait or Saudi Arabia, to ridding the area of Saddam forever. With Jupiter squaring Saddam's Sun and Uranus over the fall, expect his reckless belligerence to continue. Favorable aspects will prevail for him into the early winter. But by November, Saturn will begin activating his T-Square, and by the end of the month, warlike Mars will oppose his natal Mars. If the volcano hasn't erupted yet, this should be the time.

Then again, Saddam is a pretty bright guy, and no matter how crazy, suicidal or genocidal he may be, he also knows that among his options is a negotiated settlement. He could win his biggest victory by simply redrawing the lines in the Kuwaiti sand at the bargaining table, where he could retain part of Northern Kuwait, Bubiyan and Warba islands, and the rich Rumaila oil field, giving back the rest of the country and proposing elections to choose a new government—in exchange for an evacuation of American forces from the area.

And the United States and friends must decide if the price of oil is worth the cost of blood.

But in such a turbulent climate the Persian Gulf could go up at any moment. I will be elated but surprised if there *is* a negotiated settlement to this crisis. And when the poop does indeed hit the proverbial fan, I expect it to erupt furiously, with the U.S. and MultiNational forces relentlessly taking out most of Iraq's military installations quite rapidly. It is doubtful that many of Saddam's Scud missles will penetrate our AWAC defense system, and most of his longer range liquid fuel rockets which take hours to prepare for launch won't even get off the pad.

But Saddam is a survivor, willing to take very heavy losses, and I'm sure he's quite capable of taking out some of the rich Saudi oil fields three hundred miles away, among much other damage. If he does, global economic markets will indeed go crazy. I would not be surprised to see crude oil shoot up to $50 a barrel, and the NYSE dropping to $2000, with vast and complex economic reverberations throughout the world. Japan in particular will take it squarely on the chin. If war breaks out, there will be a selective economic extinction of that which doesn't serve the future's true needs, accompanied by a rise of all that does.

And the United States and friends must decide if the price of oil is worth the cost of blood.

But by Mid-January, when lord of karma, Saturn conjoins Saddam's Jupiter and opposes his deathstar Pluto, he may very well meet his *Waterloo*. France, Israel, or even the U.S. may even pop the genie out of the bottle and nuke Iraq; afterall, Pluto does rule the nuclear bomb. But at that very same time, Saturn will conjoin the position of the U.S.'s Pluto, while Neptune opposes the U.S.'s Sun. So I would anticipate a more sober, but powerful conventional response at this time. I would also expect this to catalyze massive transformations in our entire socioeconomic structure, foreign policy, and way of life. Whether war breaks out or not, the world of the 90's promises to turn into a very different place.

But by Mid-January, when lord of karma, Saturn conjoins Saddam's Jupiter and opposes his deathstar Pluto, he may very well meet his 'Waterloo.'

But there is a flip side to the Persian Gulf crisis coin, which could result in some good news: It may serve to inadvertently help save this planet from its collision course toward self destruction! Needless industrialization is destroying our environment as mankind bolts ahead in its indescriminate scramble for wealth. Though Saddam Hussein is neither christ nor anti-christ in my book, he may just be the catalyst which slows the global economy down, forces the West to shift economic priorities to support a more functional and attuned industrialization, and provides the kick in the rear our alternative energy effort so desperately needs. The growing environmental movement which at least got a propoganda boost from *Earth Day* in 1990, should really catch fire in 1991. This crisis should elevate retrofitting for alternative energy sources back to a higher priority. Even if this crisis is somehow diffused, it's high time our government adopted a Manhattan-Project mentality toward developing renewable non-polluting sources of energy! We obviously have the need to immediately sever ourselves from the Middle

America

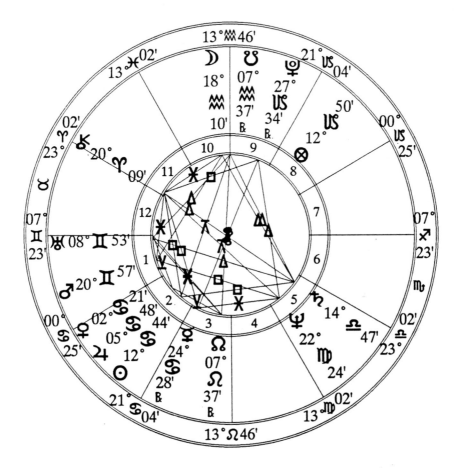

July 4, 1776
2:13:32 AM
Philadelphia, PA

114

Eastern oil teat. And one look at our arsenal of weaponry demonstrates that we certainly have the technology, the funds, the manpower, and the brains to make whatever changes are necessary. It's just a question of the *vision* thing. Energy flows to this Earth from the Sun at a constant rate of 170 billion megawatts a day, or about 25,000 times total global energy demands. And *all* of the nonrenewable energy we use is equivalent to only a couple of days worth of solar energy! With some ingenuity in redesigning and retrofitting existing structures, solar energy could cleanly and cost effectively meet *all* of the one-fourth of the U.S. energy budget which now goes into space heating and cooling. It has only been the political self interest of oil lobby politicians, corporate stubbornness, and a blindness of vision in our leadership which has retarded our progress in this area.

Energy flows to this Earth from the Sun at a constant rate of 170 billion megawatts a day or about 25,000 times total global energy demands.

Perhaps we will rise from this experience with fresh new resolve. Saddam Hussein's madness may actually engender a new era, if not a new age, where the creativity of our minds, the light of our spirits, the fire in our hearts, and the will to live a grander vision will help us devise genuine links with a future. Don't our children deserve a chance? Or will this only serve to widen the evolutionary split between those in power and those who want to live and let live.

So go out and pump up your bike tires, plant some seeds in your garden, stay healthy, fit, and happy; treasure your peace, your friends and your family, and get ready for the roller coaster ride. Think globally, act locally, but let's all get busy creating a better life for ourselves and those who dwell in our circle of light.

Some of them grew angry, by the way the Earth was abused, by the men who learned how to forge her beauty into power....

—Jackson Browne

PERSIAN GULF POSTCRIPT: 3/91

I am myself astonished that the timing and scenario of the war synchronized so well with my astrological prognostications. If nothing else, this is a very solid validation of the power of predictive astrology. But what was the score of the war? With the U.S. destroying Iraq and Saddam burning Kuwait, it looks like it was a tie, one to one; with the karma begging for a rubber match at some future date. No one can deny that we won a *military victory* in the Persian Gulf. We certainly defended Saudi Arabia and got the Iraqi military out of Kuwait, but we also opened up a Pandora's Box of Middle Eastern monsters which will we will have to try to keep at bay for many Moons. Some other war scores: Two countries destroyed, two hundred thousand Iraqi's killlled or wounded, two million Iraqi's homeless, two hundred million people distraught. Devastation abounds, anarachy has arrived, and the area is now thoroughly destabilized. Mother Earth's skies have been darkened, her eyes blackened, her sweet heart broken: Only Father Time will tell if she will heal and smile again. And we didn't even capture or punish Saddam! And you do know what Saddam spells backward don't you—Mad-as(s). One simple lesson must be crystal clear from this experience which must be learned: War is simply immature and unnacceptable for a modern civilization because it is fought between governments, not people, and because....*nobody* can really *win*.

We are almost surrounded by the whites, and it seems to be their intention to destroy us as a people.
—Dragging Canoe, 1776

117

The Gladiators Enter the Arena

(Editors Note: Astrologer *par excellance* Ken Kalb penned this
analysis, interestingly, *before* Ross Perot's recent withdrawal!)
—J.W. San Marchi, *The Voice*

Two hundred and sixteen years from our birth as a
nation, America sits at a true crossroads. With the
highest political office in the land once again up for
grabs, alignments and strategies for grabbing the proverbial
ring of power are now being forged. Will the seat of power be
retained by the status quo, or will the prevailing winds of
change bring in new leadership? Three thoroughly distinct
choices stand before the American people in selecting our

42nd president, which would lead us in three very different directions. From my highly biased view, it appears that the relection of Bush and Quayle would result in a perpetuation of the failure formula which now finds our country some $4 trillion in debt, and our environment, economy, social structure, and quality of life detiorating rapidly. A Ross Perot presidency would certainly represent a radical departure from our current course, a major cleanup of the entire governmental process, and a new relationship between government and people and business and the rest of the world. And the Clinton/Gore ticket looks like it has the potential of providing a truly inspired new generation of leadership with a detailed and viable vision of a genuinely brighter future for America. But as the campaigns crystallize over the summer and political strategies are more clearly defined, the real politics of power will be thrust into full force this fall. The parade of skeletons will waltz out of their closets and onto the dance floor as the media has its feeding frenzy and history unfolds. The current administration is certainly not going to roll over and play dead, no matter how unpopular they become or how bad the economy looks at election time. I expect some real mudwrestling, and pray that our current antiquated political processes provide enough equity to have a fair result. But during these wild times of the Uranus/Neptune conjunction in Capricorn where structures are being transformed in the *Waring Blender of change*, a wide spectrum of possible scenarios can unfold.

Many people are wondering if there will be a smooth transfer of power, or anything from assasination attempts, October surprises, or a parliamentary style selection in the revamped House of Representatives in January; resulting in an

Bill Clinton

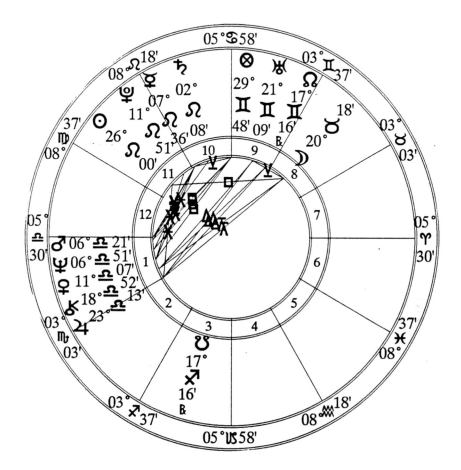

August 19, 1946
8:51 AM
Hope, AR

120

unpopular President with a mandate of only one third of the people, with the other two thirds being very pissed off. What began as a foregone conclusion of four more years of Bush and Quayle has turned about into a wild three-way horse race in a dead heat. So let's look to the stars for some other insights into these candidates and related issues in this preliminary look at the AstroPolitics of 1992.

The three candidates come from three different astrological elements: Bush (Gemini) and Quayle (Aquarius) are air signs. Perot (Cancer) a water sign, and Clinton (Leo) and Gore (Aries) fire signs. A slightly closer look finds George Bush a Gemini with Virgo rising and a Libra Moon, and Dan Quayle an Aquarian with Gemini rising and a Leo Moon. Ross Perot is a triple Cancer; that's right, his Sun, Moon, and rising sign are all in the sign of Cancer! Bill Clinton is a Leo with Libra Rising and a Taurus Moon, and Al Gore is an Aries with Leo Rising and a Capricorn Moon.

The double—double airsign attack of Bush/Quayle should be filled with alot of highly charged rhetoric which has little to do with much besides proselytizing for political advantage, celebratory backpats for past international exploits, including taking credit for ending the cold war, negative politicking, self-immolation, and promises. The tidal wave of Ross Perot should be very strong, unpredicable, and tempermental as he faces the new challenges of constantly answering to the myopic media and getting himself to put up with the political process. But I would not be surprised if very suddenly Mr. triple-Crab plunges back in his shell after some more barbecues on the political grill and pulls out of the race. But with the Uranus/Neptune conjunction in Capricorn opposing all of his Cancer planets, Perot will be hot-wired

Al Gore

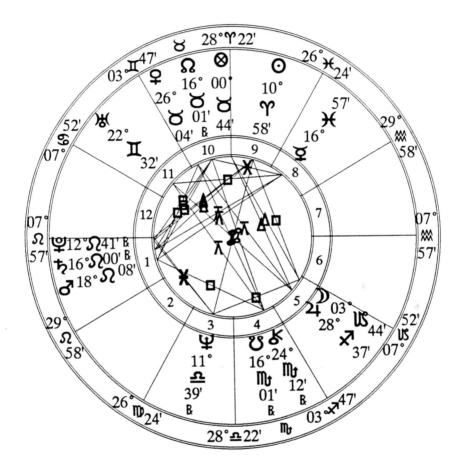

March 31, 1948
12:53 PM
Carthage, TN

122

into the revolutionary nature of the times. The double firesign blaze of the young democrats will be very hard to slow down. The synergy of Clinton and Gore's charts makes each of them stronger, and the democrats, so very hungry to take charge amidst the current potential vulnerability, will prove formidable adversaries for the status quo. They are sure to stir our spirits with a powerful dose of fresh optimism about their various ideas for restoring some sanity and hope for the future of American Life.

But I would not be surprised if very suddenly Mr. triple-Crab plunges back in his shell after some more barbecues on the political grill and pulls out of the race.

The question of the vice presidency may be the key to victory. There are many who feel that the ticket should be reversed, with the Arien Gore taking the lead, supported by the lion, Mr. Clinton. In any event, the idea of Gore being only a heartbeat away from a President Clinton is far more palatable to many undecided's than a possible President Quayle. A President Stockdale would be unconscionable, so go ahead and forget about a President Perot. He's in this for another purpose.

The Geminian nature of the United States is reflected in the polarity of the two party system. The Perot factor is testimony that people are no longer identifying with traditional bipartisanship and are thoroughly disgruntled with the status quo. With the triple conjunction in 1993 of the

George Bush

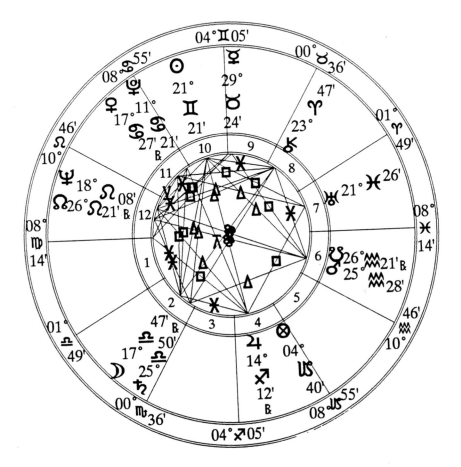

June 12, 1924
11:30 AM
Milton, MA

124

outer planetary giants Uranus and Neptune, America will unconsciously, be in full revolutionary metamorphosis. With Gemini rising in America's chart, we certainly do appear to be two countries with two value systems running at cross purposes. Just like our heritage of revolting from the Mother Country, or our Civil War, we our at odds with our very selves. Who America really is, that is which side is the stronger, will tip the balance of power in its direction, perhaps just in the nick of time.

In Part II of this series, we'll look more specifically at the candidates, the current and progressed charts of the United States, the movements of the outer planets and their influences on the country and candidates and several related issues. For now, take a peek at our candidates charts, and deepen your insights into the personalities illuminated in the political spotlight.

I hope I have stirred your political pot enough to get your stew simmering. And however you feel about our country or these candidates, please get out and talk about how you feel, and be sure to vote—it's the most powerful political statement we can make.

American Astropolitics—Part II
The Transfer of Power in the Waring Blender of Change

Here we are friends, twenty centuries after the birth of Jesus Christ, rapidly closing in on a third millennium, in the last five weeks of a power struggle for the most powerful position of the most powerful country on our wonderful planet. With revolutionary Uranus and mysterious Neptune aligned in Capricorn—sign of structure and government—opposing America's Sun (essence) and squaring America's Saturn (structure), we are whirling through the wacky transformative process of revising ourselves. Now that summer has become fall, and Uranus and Neptune have shifted from retrograde to direct, the *Waring Blender of change* has moved from puree up to whip, with its yellow *system failure* light flashing at quickening intervals.

Just picture James Baker sitting at his desk in the Western chambers of the White House, feet perched on his desk, pencil tapping, plotting out these final weeks of the campaign. With Bush behind, its time to pull out the heavy artillery—perhaps some type of October Surprise? We'll get to see just what political muscles flex up the long sleeves of those in the seat of power, and if they're strong and coordinated enough to reverse the ebbing political tide? Or is it now just a foregone conclusion after the calamitous Republican convention that the party needs to go back to its drawing board for four years, with Bush going down a loser? What possible scenarios and strategies are flashing through this master strategist's eye:

A. Suck Clinton into a debate format stacked in Bush's favor to rise up to parity from underdog, and set a trap to drop new character bombshells.

B. Create a crisis—like new instability in the ex-Soviet Union. It certainly worked in the Persian Gulf to elevate Bush's 43 percent approval rating up to 92 percent !

C. Try to capture Saddam Hussein and bring him back to the United Nations for War Tribunals, with the nation once again rallying around the incumbent flagbearer?

D. Invite Perot into the fold whenever possible, since the Perot factor takes anti-Bush votes away from Clinton.

E. Massage October 27th's economic numbers to look like the recovery is at hand.

F. Use the awesome power of the incumbency to its full extent.

Whatever become the ingredients of the strategy, the fight to the finish will be intensifying to full hurricane strength.

Meanwhile, Mr. TripleCrab, political wildcard Ross Perot has incubated long enough in his lavish carapace. A short campaign couldn't be too traumatic now that he has manipulated his own ground rules, including answering the media only on certain issues. Claiming he doesn't really want the job, but is rather being *called to service* to force the deficit-reduction issue and break government gridlock, he is nobly responding to the cause with his blunt blitz of down-home style direct solutions. With his name on the ballot in all fifty states, Mr. Perot will pop out of his shell and run like hell for awhile. Even if he doesn't run, he really is running—and will get the *none of the above votes*, the *I'm made as hell....* votes, as well as the support of his loyalists. Certainly the Bush camp is celebrating Mr. Perot's reentry, as a rocking boat will beat a sinking ship on any day.

So let's check out the astrological backdrop, then examine certain features of the birthchart of the United States and its relation to the upcoming planetary movements and influences for the astropolitical surf forecast.

America was born from a Revolutionary War just when there were upheavals in France and many other countries in

Dan Quayle

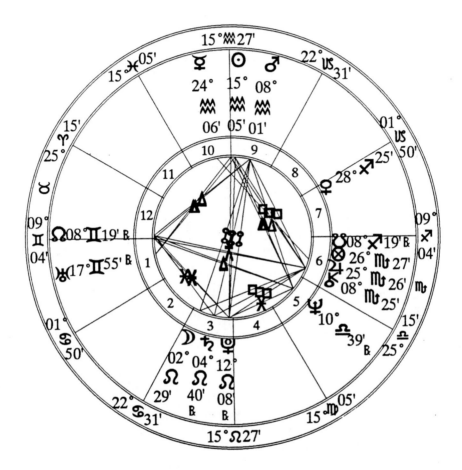

February 4, 1947
12:00 PM
Indianapolis, Indiana

synchronicity with the actual time of the discovery of the planet Uranus. This planet, ruled by Aquarius, has come to signify revolution, innovation, discovery, change, the new, and unusual. It is a very diffent archetype than Saturn, ruler of Capricorn, which represents the old, time, tradition, rules, laws, government, stability, and structure. Whenever Uranus makes a conjunction to a major planet there is a revolution in that planet's realm; when Uranus goes through a sign, the nature of matters in that sign undergo a metamorphosis. Uranus in Capricorn means structural revolution, and since its entry four years ago much of the global map has been redrawn. Slow moving Neptune represents faith, mysticism, and the higher octave of creativity on the light side; escapism, fantasy, drugs, deception, and dissolution on the darker. Aligned with Uranus in Capricorn, there is an amplifying and blending of their energies all through 1993; a real cosmic hurricane swirling through the universal unconscious. This once every 171-year phenomena has never happened before during modern times. Their current position in mid-Capricorn places them in direct opposition to America's Sun during our country's birth. They are also in a precise *square* to the position Saturn occupied (in mid-Libra) in America's chart. Synchronous with all of these *hard* aspects, America finds itself in a deepening multidimensional crisis of unparalleled magnitude in its 216-year history, where we are being forced to revise ourselves, or our system fails. This Presidential election is really about whether we continue to let the wheels fall off until we crash, or we opt to get very busy making some major changes.

So the universe has gone ahead and signaled for our second American Revolution by immersing us in the

Ross Perot

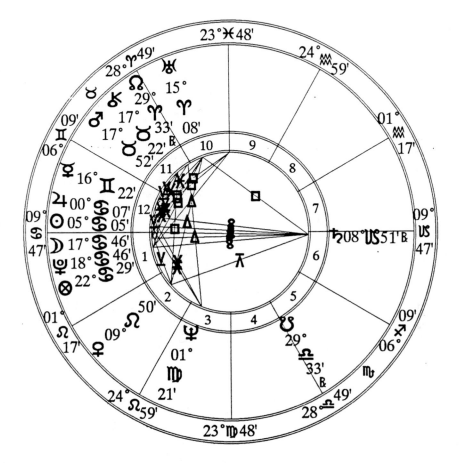

June 27, 1930
5:34 AM
Texarkana, AR

awareness of the urgency for a top to bottom revision of everything from our very lives to our society, and especially our overgrown and failing political processes and institutions.

When the Moon is full it is always opposite the Sun—a time of heightened awareness and intensity. When planets are in opposition, they have a *full Moon* effect on each other. Ross Perot's heavy Cancerian makeup is in direct opposition to the Uranus/Neptune conjunction, making him the perfect ambassador for discontent with the system and its dubious leaders. Not only does his Moon conjoin America's Sun—showing an intimate connection with the country's essence (the American Dream?)—but it will be in direct opposition to Uranus and Neptune on election day. Little wonder this enigmatic, unpredictable, and zany character is in the center of the political cyclone.

The Moon is the most sensitive point in the birthchart defining one's environment from the smallest unit—the cell—to the largest—the universal.

Most fascinating is how all three candidates have their Moons at the 17th degree—Perot in Cancer, Bush in Libra, and Clinton in Taurus. On election day, Neptune will be at the 17th degree of Capricorn with Uranus right next door at the 15th: Opposing Perot's Moon, Squaring Bush's Moon, and Trining Clinton's. The Moon is the most sensitive point in the birthchart defining one's environment from the smallest unit—the cell, to the largest—the universal. Perot's

Jerry Brown

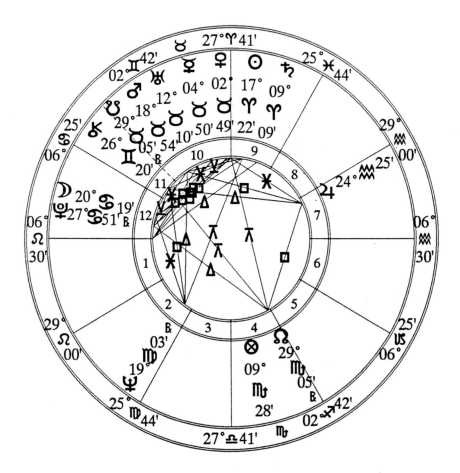

April 7, 1938
12:34 PM
Los Angeles, California

132

lunar opposition to Uranus and Neptune wires him into his tempestuous, downright ornery, revolutionary and innovative role; *and* explains his frequent disappearing acts due to the Neptunian dissolution effect. Bush's lunar square to Neptune has been synchronous with his weakening popularity and influence as well as the perception of his deception, making it hard for him to be in touch with the pulse of the people, or reality, for that matter. Uranus squaring his Moon increases tensions, upsets and instability; an erratic time of inconsistent changes. In contrast, Clinton has been enjoying favorable trines from these two aligned giants—increasing his compassion, intuition, and empathy, and his ability to ride the waves of change gracefully and positively. The Universe is indeed pumping favorable winds into Clinton's hoisted sail, while Perot bounces off the Walls, and Bush flounders in the perilous Horse latitudes. So get ready to be deluged by the Air Attack of Bush and Quayle, the Water Wiggle of Perot and Stockdale, and the Fire Brigade of Clinton and Gore at full bore until you finally cast your critical vote.

Since its World Series time, let's think in terms of baseball for a historical perspective. The score is 10 to nothing, there's two out in the bottom of the ninth inning, with Darth Vader on the mound for the Power Structure: looking awfully bleak for the People . . . except . . . Yoda is at bat. May the force be with us!

Around the next Full Moon, Jupiter, our largest planet and ruler of growth, benevolence, luck, and optimism enters the Venusian sign of Libra for a year. Twelve years ago, when Reagan and Bush were elected, Jupiter had also entered Libra, so this could mark the completion of their cycle. Furthermore, Clinton has four planets in Libra, including his Jupiter—so this timely Jupiter return now will provide another big boost. Does this mean an easy Clinton/Gore victory. Hardly. Then who will win? Sorry friends, I'm still building more suspense prior to my prognostication.

Pay attention to these politicians and look at their charts, because with the exception of Bush, they will all be back in intensified and reinvented form in the wild political arena of 1996.

What this election boils down to is a classic battle of old and new, status quo against change, power vs. the people, older generation/younger generation, Saturn and Jupiter. The charts even find President Bush's Saturn at 25 degrees Libra aligned with Governor Clinton's Jupiter at 23 degrees of Libra! And with America's Saturn in Libra, the battle lines could not be more clearly drawn. Since its World Series time, let's think in terms of baseball for a historical perspective. The score is 10 to nothing, there's two out in the bottom of the ninth inning, with Darth Vader on the mound for the Power Structure: looking awfully bleak for the People . . . except . . . Yoda is at bat. May the force be with us!

Hillary Clinton

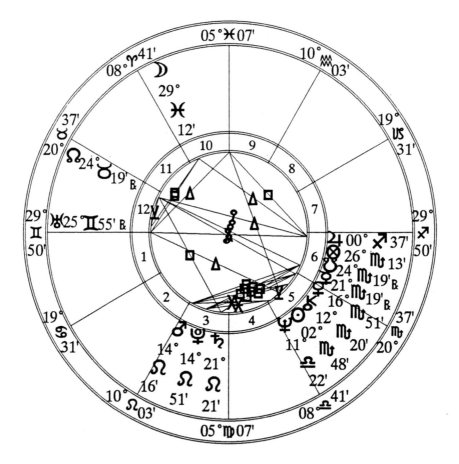

October 26, 1947
8:00 PM
Chicago, IL

Pay attention to these politicians and look at their charts, because with the exception of Bush, they will *all* be back in intensified and reinvented form in the wild political arena of 1996.

Another feature of this election is the generational struggle and the Saturnian quality of being stubborn about letting go and trusting in the future (Jupiter). Bush (and Perot) were born around the depression when Pluto was in Cancer. This generation is very security-minded, with experiences like the Great Depression, World War II, post-war military industrialization, and a very different world of many less people and seemingly unlimited resources as major character molding experiences and climates. Clinton and Gore are from the Pluto in Leo generation of the PostWar: Sixties people who have come of age and matured. This generation is concerned with creating a healthy and happy future where people can flourish into the future at their highest potentials in a clean environment. Isn't it interesting how the Draft for The Vietnam War which the Pluto in Cancer generation tried to force their Pluto in Leo children to fight, became one of this campaign's biggest non-issues.

So get ready to be deluged by the Air Attack of Bush and Quayle, the Water Wiggle of Perot and Stockdale, and the Fire Brigade of Clinton and Gore at full bore until you finally cast your critical vote.

And what about the *year of the Woman*? This is where Clinton and Gore really score—and not just because they're young and cute. Amidst a a pathetic economy, Bush is foolish to embrace his *Pro-Life* position which 78 percent of the country opposes. Women do make up 52 percent, the largest block of voters. Clinton and Gore both have their Progressed Suns crossing Venus in their birthcharts which may account for their attunement to women's concerns. President Bush was born with his Moon square Venus (problems with women), and with Neptune squaring his Moon, he is *really* spaced-out right now. *He* must have been the one who sicced Quayle on Murphy Brown. Then again, Dan does have his difficulties getting his M & M's in alphabetical order!

On Election day, the Sun will Square Saturn, just as it did on July 4th of 1776. America will have a lunar return and the Moon will be in late Aquarius (ruled by revolutionary Uranus), right where it was during our country's birth. Are these indications that this election is indeed pointing toward a Second Revolution? But the Moon will be *Void of Course* during most of the day, which could signal circumstances like problems voting, voter indecision, an upset, or no clear winner setting up a constitutional crisis for the new House of Representatives. Perhaps this would be just the predicament we need to proceed with the screw top, ziplock surgery we require. In the *Waring Blender of Change*, anything is possible. But most likely I think the *Fire Brigade* will be elected to deal with the big blazes they will find in their faces during our *Grand Catharsis* ahead.

I never apologize for the United States of America.
I don't care what the facts are   —George Bush

The Signs of the Presidents

ARIES	2	Thomas Jefferson, John Tyler
TAURUS	4	James Monroe, Ulysses Grant, James Buchanan, Harry Truman
GEMINI	2	John Kennedy, George Bush
CANCER	3	John Q. Adams, Calvin Coolidge, Gerald Ford
LEO	3	Benjamin Harrison, Herbert Hoover, Bill Clinton
VIRGO	2	William Taft, Lyndon Johnson
LIBRA	4	Rutherford Hayes, Chester Arthur, Dwight Eisenhower, Jimmy Carter
SCORPIO	5	John Adams, James Polk, James Garfield, Theodore Roosevelt, Warren Harding
SAGITTARIUS	3	Martin Van Buren, Zachary Taylor, Franklin Pierce
CAPRICORN	3	Millard Filmore, Andrew Johnson, Woodrow Wilson
AQUARIUS	5	William Harrison, Abraham Lincoln, William McKinley, Franklin Roosevelt, Ronald Reagan
PISCES	4	George Washington, James Madison, Andrew Jackson, Grover Cleveland

★ 10 ★

The Grand Catharsis Formula

Originally Published March 1993

A re you feeling just a bit bizarre these days, or is business just usual for you? Though celestial influences affect each of us differently, I would be very surprised if you aren't busy reinventing yourself in very significant ways right now. And that particular project is certainly the *Mother* of all Invention.

You've heard me discuss the conjunction of giants Uranus and Neptune in Capricorn many times. Some of you are probably also aware of the approaching squares of Saturn in Aquarius to Pluto in Scorpio or its opposition to Chiron in Leo; Jupiter's retrograde in Libra, or Mar's retrograde/direct shifts in Cancer. This week, Mercury and Pluto will go retrograde, and the Moon is in one of Carl Payne Tobey's

Wobbles. No, the Universe is not ganging up on us in some sort of celestial plot. Nor do I interpret these planetary phenomenon as being negative or bad. Bizarre, chaotic, creative, intuitive, inventive, enigmatic, and transformative, to be sure. In fact, I call this phase in Earth history, *The Grand Catharsis.* But this three year cycle will clear the way for the long awaited and much heralded Aquarian period ahead.

Wherever Uranus makes a conjunction to a major planet there is a metamorphosis in the matters of that planet's domain. There is hyperawareness and sensitivity, intensification and amplification. Kind of like turning on the power booster to a car stereo. Uranus, higher octave of Mercury electrifies or *wires,* if you will; Neptune, higher octave of Venus magnetizes or *pulls.* Action, reaction, synthesis— catharsis, metamorphosis. The Moth in chrysalis becomes a butterfly. In what form will you emerge from your once comfortable cacoon? I'd advise just letting this entire process unfold one day at a time!

The word power is not normally associated with the planet Neptune. In fact, it is a power vacuum, a worm hole, a dissolver, a fantasizer, an artist, an escape artist.

The word power is not normally associated with the planet Neptune. In fact, it is a power vacuum, a worm hole, a dissolver, a fantasizer, an artist, an escape artist. Mystical, magical, spiritual, wordless, timeless, sometimes bizarre, always a bit weird. A mystic yogi doing sadhana in the Himalayas; a Grateful Deadhead doing acid in the Rockies; a Fellini Movie. A stroll through Alice's Wonderland, a Pan-Galactic gargle blaster at the Star Wars Bar, or trying to tell time on a Salvador Dali clock. The *Kronosynclasticinfandibulum*—a Kurt Vonnegut Jr. creation describing that point where space and time merge, or should I say, *melt*. As trans-Saturnian planets, Uranus, Neptune, and Pluto are part of our *Unconscious*, connecting us with all of the vast cosmic forces of the rest of the Universe; so it is this powerful and intangible dimension of our being which is engaged in the process of *Grand Catharsis*.

Uranus is like a lightning storm, where the contagion of electrical energy creates a vortex of creative change. Brilliant flashes of inspiration, sudden transformative insights, instant unexpected changes from out of the blue—these are things Uranian. Thomas Edison inventing the incandescent bulb, a Close Encounter of the Third Kind. A volcanic eruption, a discovery, a breakthrough. Meeting someone new, being spontaneous, following your instincts.

Uranus is like a lightning storm, where the contagion of electrical energy creates a vortex of creative change.

The wedding bells of the Uranus-Neptune marriage herald magnificent Renaissance possibilities. Music, literature, the arts, film, architecture, technology, and medicine should all flourish. But the divorce proceedings from the past present other scenarios of anarchy, chaos, social disorder, accidents, cataclysms, and bizarre incidents.

Your personal changes may seem subtle on a day to day basis. Are your dreams getting more vivid, are you having trouble sleeping; are you day-dreaming or day-tripping perhaps? Are you finding yourself in multi-tangential conversations? Then again, direct Uranus/Neptune contacts may electromagnetically thrust you into much more abrupt changes. So if circumstances seem to guide you, or you simply feel like starting that new rock band, becoming a healer, building electric cars, quitting that stodgy old job and starting your own enterprise, joining an alternative community, moving to the country—making that *long* awaited change; just let it happen. Live your (im)possible dream! What is indeed going on is a cresting wave of consciousness cracking your cosmic egg. Just have faith that all will turn out sunny-side up. During its last conjunction 171 years ago, they called this the *Age of Enlightenment*. And life on our planet has certainly taken a broad jump since then. I wonder what history will call our *current* quantum leap in its retrospective analysis? Maybe.......*The Grand Catharsis*.

It is precisely the direction of that last jump which needs correction at this time. Populations have increased too fast. Our social, political, economic, legal, and environmental systems are all on overload. The wild and greedy scramble for wealth and power which has accompanied the industrial and technological revolutions and population explosions have created massive imbalances. From A to Z there is truly very little in the quality of life on a collective level—as a society, a country, or world which is truly improving. Thank God we have the ability to transform our personal universes and create

Mohatma Ghandi

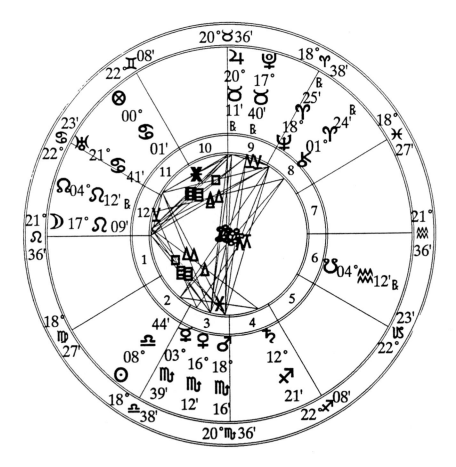

October 2, 1869
2:30 AM
Porbrandar, India

positive and fullfilling lives! This is a most critical point to consider: The dichotomy between the personal and the collective grows larger. While we can most certainly create good lives for ourselves, our families and our friends; society and particularly government is a very different story. Will the catharses be grand enough to turn around the wretched excesses of modern civilization? So while the grandest of juries sequesters in deliberation on that question, the best place we can put our delicate eggs is in the basket of our love—the *only* real part of our lives.

With giant of giants Jupiter in the Venusian sign of balance, Libra this year, major revisions and adjustments in relationships are transpiring. At the core, Venus represents our values, so with the glowing Jupiterian light illuminating what we truly care about, perhaps life, liberty and the pursuit of happiness; love, peace, and health will regain the top priority. Peace masters Mohatma Ghandi and Jimmy Carter are solar Librians from whom we can learn alot about the art of fairness. Libra also strives to maintain balance, so getting all of the components of our lives functioning in vital harmony is our challenge for optimizing our lives. But things will undoubtedly shake up during this process of rebalancing. Jupiter's transit through the first half of Libra has rototilled the grounds for reinventing and rerooting what we value. This begins with our primary relationship—our Self—then extends to our friends, our mates, our family, the community, our work, and our world. During the second half of Libra this summer and fall, we will connect up on a new and improved level with all of the components which are to become the new parts of our upgraded lives. By the time

Jimmy Carter

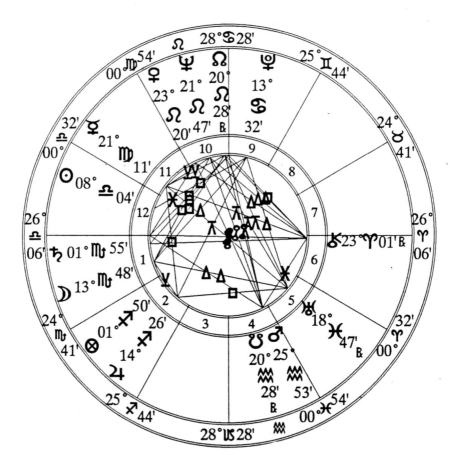

October 1, 1924
7:00 AM
Plains, GA

Jupiter reaches Scorpio and eliminates, focuses, transforms and purifies the multiple Librien options, what we truly stand for and who we stand with should be more clearly on target.

The cards are being shuffled in the relationship deck right now, because so many of us are going through big shifts while we are also redefining what we really want in our reinvented lives. But this is also to be expected during a Neptune (dissolving) conjunction with Uranus (friendships) as well. For many of us, our new path may be for our steps alone for awhile, until we park in new orbits circumscribed around the upgraded dimensions of ourselves.

The cards are being shuffled in the relationship deck right now, because so many of us are going through big shifts while we are also redefining what we really want in our reinvented lives..

The Saturn-Pluto squares of the spring and fall present major challenges for transformation on both personal and political fronts. For you and I, it is a time to create a success formula and a breakthrough from a significant hangup hanging around for the last 7 years or so. Some shadowy habit or pattern needs to be exposed, released, transformed and healed setting us free to be more free.

On the political front, Pluto will square President Clinton's Sun while Saturn will oppose it. Our new President has been riding a big wave of luck and charisma, enjoying a Jupiter return in his charming Librien first house—as well as Jupiter's conjunction with his Venus, Mars, Neptune, and

Ascendant. But the hard Pluto and Saturn transits are bound to flatten some of the tires on the Clinton bus. This Jupiter influence accounts for his daring to disregard certain campaign promises, or to try to raise taxes right at tax time. Gridlock will return in its greatest glory at times as certain agenda items like the Clinton economic or health programs get transformed on Capitol Hill creating one grandly cathartic mess. But after the smoke clears, far bolder solutions should eventually emerge. Pluto in Scorpio will return to square President Clinton's Leonian natal Sun through most of 1994, so he should face many challenges, enemies, scandals, and skeletons from his past; a very rough journey. If he survives this onslaught into 1995 when Pluto enters Sagittarius, he will have been transformed and forged into a very strong leader. If not, perhaps we might just find his fire brother vice president at the helm of our nation.

Or, as Ross Perot says, is that like giving an alcholic a charge account at a liquor store and asking him to only buy the peanuts.

I expect a similar scenario with the Rodney King trial this spring. Bad news and powerful reactions which create emergency situations will result in forcing us to get real and make geniune changes. Do you think government is actually capable of getting control of itself—to start functioning efficiently and effectively for the true good of the people? Or, as Ross Perot says, is that like giving an alcoholic a charge account at a liquor store and asking him to only buy the peanuts. But at least our new President has thrown the fat onto the fire so the economy and some other important issues can sizzle on the political grill for awhile. And either the economy, the political structure, or both, and our relationship to government will eventually undergo a true grand catharsis grappling with these issues.

But it won't be until the day when we fully revise and devise governmental structures where people truly feel connected again to government; where we feel like we have a meaningful voice in our self-governance as a positive force in our lives, that we complete our catharsis. And that will be a happy day, and it may end up not being all that far away.

Isn't it amazing how falling on our faces sometimes makes us get much smarter?

Wouldn't it be great if we solved our problems simply from awareness with swift action. It would even be all right if we responded rapidly to emergencies with solutions. Unfortunately, it is only in the face of catastrophe that we seem to respond boldly and decisively. Isn't it amazing how falling on our faces sometimes makes us get much smarter? But this is one of key ingredients of the grand catharsis formula during this period: Breakthroughs to success emerging from our failures; responses to catastrophe amidst a climate of intense change and inspiration. That's when the human spirit pulls out all the stops and shows its true light and real worth. And since we are heading into such fiercely challenging territory ahead, you can expect to see lots of true light lighting up the way out of the the amorphous and confused Piscean abyss.

Astrological tradition has always considered Neptune and Pisces to rule the twelfth house, which in its negative manifestation is the realm of self undoing and karmic debts. So is it any wonder at the end of this age that we have almost completely come undone?

Back in the future dwells some very good news which helps put this current 3-year cycle in perspective. The faster moving Uranus is enlightening the way into a more benevolent Aquarius by 1996. And by then, Pluto will have completed its complex 13-year Scorpionic cycle of deaths and rebirths and enter Sagittarius. Jupiter will have illuminated and blessed 1995 in its domicile sign of Sagittarius. And Saturn will begin a fresh new cycle in the spring of `96 when it enters Aries. Translation: the *true Aquarian period* will have arrived! Just imagine the shift in vibrational energy and consciousness from Uranus in Capricorn and Pluto in Scorpio—to Uranus in Aquarius and Pluto in Sagittarius! Cleansed from 3 years in the washing machine of the Grand Catharsis, we will emerge to a true New Age. No, the Moon will not be in the Seventh House, nor will Jupiter be aligned with Mars. And though love will most certainly continue to steer the stars, world peace and the end of human suffering may take a few Aquarian years to fully evolve and resolve.

If you've been striving for the miraculous, you will find it in the moments of your daily life!

After all, ages do last over 2000 years. But the beginning of 1997 finds Jupiter conjoining Uranus in Aquarius heralding a period of magnificent breakthroughs in medicine, technology, music, the arts, education, health, food and energy sources, among many other areas. If you've been striving for the miraculous, you will find it in the moments of your daily life! The inhabitants of this planet will be much more wide awake. Our children will amaze us as the passion in their hearts, the genius of their minds, and the wisdom of their ancient souls creates a viable future from their powerful will to live and the response it engenders from their post-war parents. By 1998 Neptune will join Uranus in Aquarius and our lives, our community, and our world will enter the third millenium quite thoroughly transformed.

Remember, we are in the final three years of a two thousand year Piscean cycle. The start/finish line of a fresh new period for humanity is coming into focus. So ride with these current waves of change, because you are preparing yourself for a period much more in tune with the magnificent potential of the human spirit and the destiny of mankind.

Smile at me, spirit in me living let your Presence guide my destiny....Smile at me 'cause there's Light in me giving all the strength and love and life I need to be....

—Flaming Arrow

Surrender

As I sit back and surrender
to the Sun's exalted kiss
and dream in awe and splendor
And feel life's happiness
To know the spiraling joys and sorrows
quivering up my spine
And the magical paths Time leads me
On this ladder to the divine
A few steps broken here and there
a few valleys are bare
Just an acid test of faith
for the golden goal we share
A bird sings love to a tree
a butterfly lights on me
A shooting star in the night
makes me stand upright.
A rivers lifegift I take to my lips
I'm caressed by the water of life.
A deep breathe of aromatic scent Osmoses
and I become One with love from Thee
So soft and gentle
sweet and fresh
pure and holy
proud and strong
are thee....

✫ ✫

SuperConjunction 1994

Originally
Published
December 1993

This New Year will rock and roll here with the closest planetary alignment in several hundred years. On January 11th, seven planets will all conjoin within just 9 degrees in the Saturn-ruled Cardinal Earth sign, Capricorn. The sign of the Winter Solstice, Christmas, Ben Franklin, Yogananda, Martin Luther King, and ok—Richard Nixon and Rush Limbaugh, among many others. Yes the Sun, Moon, Mercury, Venus and Mars are all lining up at the precise point where distant giants Uranus and Neptune have been making their rare rendezvous all year. The conjunction, the most powerful of astrological aspects, marks the beginning of a new cycle, like the New Moon every month which always conjoins the Sun. Now, with 7 planets closely aligned (and over 20 actual conjunctions and parallels), this New Year is

SuperConjunction 1994

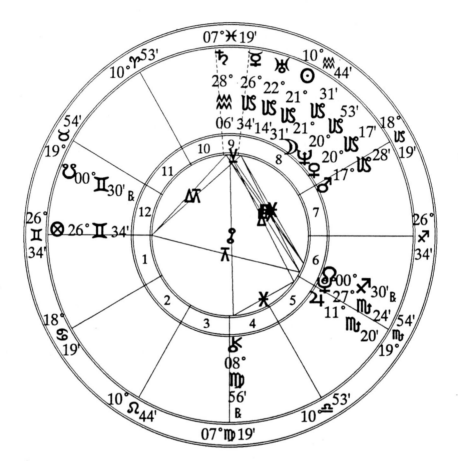

January 11, 1994
3:10 PM
Santa Barbara, CA

153

truly the start of a fresh cycle for all planetary residents, and a splendid way for God to celebrate the two thousandth birthday of Jesus Christ, and the joyous & vibrant spirit within each and every one of our hearts and souls which has been our birthright since the beginning of Time.

This New Year will rock and roll here with the closest planetary alignment in several hundred years.

It is quite fascinating that the only planets outside this conjunction are transformational Pluto in the sign of its rulership, Scorpio, amplified by the approaching King of planets Jupiter also in Scorpio—directly squaring off Lord of Karma Saturn, the ruler of Capricorn; the sign where the 7 planets of the Superconjunction are all aligning! Conjunctions, squares, and oppositions are the so-called *hard* aspects, so one powerful planetary train is whistle-stopping through Capricorn, a sign most seriously concerned about getting busy getting things planned and performed in harmony with the dictates of what has transculturally become known as karma.

This is the third and final square of Saturn and Pluto, with the faster moving Saturn moving ahead to Pisces by February. This square has been begging us all to clear up karma, to transform certain stuck patterns in our lives so we can break through and move forward in a more attuned manner. Just where this superconjunction and the Saturn/Pluto square contact your chart and what it means for you is something you should know about, so I suggest you

Martin Luther King

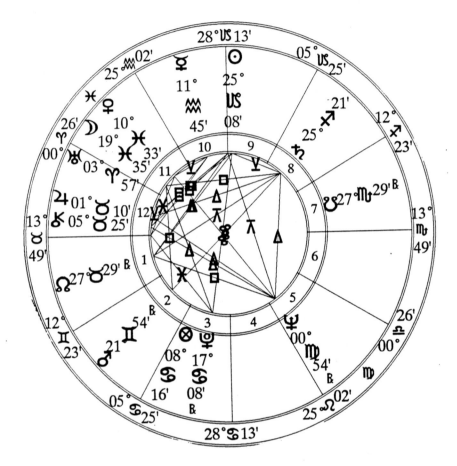

January 15, 1929
12:00 PM
Atlanta, GA

take yourself into the shop for your favorite form of astrological tune-up at this juncture.

Saturn and Pluto's T-Square to Michael Jackson's Mars, then Mercury was certainly synchronous with some new developments in *his* life. It will be most interesting to see what happens when Saturn opposes his Pluto come mid-February and conjoins his Moon in early May. I expect Mr. Jackson to lay pretty low during most of 1994 until he resurfaces in more conservative and reinvented form. Saturn and Pluto's 3 T-squares to Bill Clinton's Sun have been synchronous with mounds of kryptonite landing in his lap, including this messy Whitewater meteorite. But while the Saturn aspects are separating, the Pluto squares will continue, so expect our charismatic President to be dodging stinging bullets and jumping tall hurdles all year, but probably somewhat successfully despite these challenges.

So get ready and get set to go. This will be the year you will get clear, focused, and into gear. This is the time when all of the unconscious stirrings and longings of this bizarre Uranus/Neptune period should crystallize into a plan of action. This should be just the prescription to cure any anxiety-ridden PSS (Pre-Shift Syndrome) you may have been experiencing. Rather than just thinking or dreaming about new possibilities, affirmative plans of action should be designed and mobilized as this new cycle dawns in our lives.

January 11th, 1994 at 3:10 pm is an excellent time to make a wish from the deepest part of your heart, and then proceed in the moments and days ahead to make it happen.

You see, Uranus and Neptune are slow moving trans-Saturnian gas giants far off in the outer reaches of our Solar System, and thus, metaphysically submerged in the archetypes

Rush Limbaugh

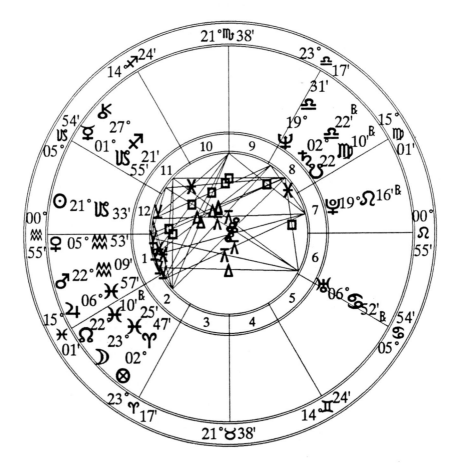

January 12, 1951
7:50 AM
Cape Garadeau, MO

of our vast Unconscious. Conversely, the faster moving inner planets, physically composed of solid matter, represent our subconscious (Moon), conscious (Sun), communicative (Mercury), and personal (Venus and Mars) modalities internally. This linkage of unconscious, subconsious, conscious, and personal—of higher and lower octaves during the Superconjunction—should now blend into a sweet and rich melody from the scattered and bizarre voices from the distance. May the song in your heart sing loud and clear this new year.

January 11th, 1994 at 3:10 pm is an excellent time to make a wish from the deepest part of your heart, and then proceed in the moments and days ahead to make it happen.

A closer look at this Superconjunction New Moon chart finds the alignment clustering principally in the 8th house (here in Santa Barbara); Scorpio's domain of sex, birth, death, rebirth and transformation, *deep*, sometimes dark territory. Bear in mind, the planets will align in different houses at different locations. Saturn-ruled Capricorn's keyword is *I Use*, with key qualities being down to earth practicality, patience, perseverence, integrity, activity, methodical planning, ambition, and structure.

Sun conjunct Moon marks a union of emotions and will, a new zeal for life, a green light; conjunct Mercury links the mind and ego, a time of willpower; conjunct Venus, a love for life; conjunct Mars, an aggressive decisive nature; conjunct

Michael Jackson

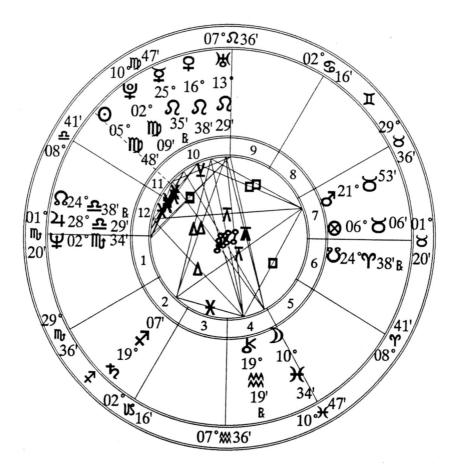

August 29 1958
11:00 AM
Gary, Indiana

Uranus, an individualistic spontaneous new approach; conjunct Neptune, heightened sensitivity and intuition. The lunar conjunctions to these planets indicate adaptability, intense feelings, sensitivity, awakening, and acting on feelings. The Mercury conjunctions indicate a sharp wit, a peaceful harmony between conscious and subconscious, perhaps even a brilliance and imaginative sensitivity in words or music. The Venusian and Martian conjunctions promise passion, personal magnetism, sparkling personality, and sex appeal. The Uranus and Neptune conjunctions linkage these personal urges with deeper dreamings, longings, and awakenings. And the entire alignment promises the potential of a new cycle which commences by focusing all of this into your everyday life. The Saturn/Pluto square poses a challenge to transform the structures in your life so you can now grow beyond your current limitations into new and grander dimensions of your self.

Those of you who have read my *Grand Planetary Alignment* or Gribbin and Plagemann's *The Jupiter Effect* may be curious about such matters as increased solar activity from the tidal influence of such a powerful alignment on the Sun, and the possible influence on terrestrial weather and seismicity. I would say a *window of vulnerability* is definitely *wide* open for Earth changes and severe weather during this period. The inner planets have been swarming in ever closer alignments to the Sun throughout the eclipse and hard-aspect acceleration phase of the Fall and Winter of '93, culminating in the upcoming Superconjunction; and the cataclysmic Southern California fires and floods were certainly synchronous. But, while Earth changes may indeed be imminent, I see this Capricorn alignment as more of an internal *KarmaQuake*. Changes in the dense mass of the physical plane are usually the last place they transpire, but physical adjustments at this time may be necessary. I have always felt the upcoming May 4th of 2000 Superconjunction to be the ripest time for the *Big One* amongst other natural rearrangements, though many strong *warning shots* will be fired first. While acute planetary alignments during sunspot maximums have proven their validity to me, geology truly has its own private agenda.

I would say a 'window of vulnerability' is definitely wide open for Earth changes and severe weather during this period.

More articles have been written about the Uranus/Neptune conjunction than any other astrological phenomena I've witnessed, yet few have been able to hit the mark because of the Unconscious nature of these planet's modus operandi. Looking back to historical antecedents will do little for understanding what is going on now. We live in a thoroughly unique set of planetary and societal circumstances as the third Millennium dawns, with 5 times as many inhabitants dwelling on this planet. The polar quality of human nature is being amplified and played out in a simultaneous personal awakening of the consciousness of many, amidst the growing possibility of our collective demise. The unfolding drama here on this Earth, of the passionate human will to survive, amidst the greedy passions of the power-hungry which surely creates marvels and comforts, yet also threatens our planetary health and quality of life, will be most fascinating.

There is no doubt that Microsoft's Bill Gates was correct when he said there would be a personal computer in every home one day soon. But will the information Superhighway create a species of 21st century humanoids playing *Mortal Combat*? Will the better deal you get over the *Home Shopping Network* or your modem be worth displacing your local merchant? Will the thousands of companies listed on your newspaper's financial pages everyday ever care about anything besides economic growth no matter what the expense to the environment or quality of our lives? Will governments ever start shrinking themselves instead of our taxpaying pocketbooks? Will Rush Limbaugh and Howard Stern ever get off their ego rockets, or will millions of lost followers continue to celebrate their public mismusings and not so private parts? I imagine our current culture heroes are just symptomatic reflections of the state of American culture. Will our media ever finish its feeding frenzy on sex, death, and scandal and use its miraculous tecnology to promote human brilliance—or will we just keep getting *157 channels with nothing on*. Will the acquisition of the almighty dollar and the power it wields ever be replaced or balanced with the spirit of Love in our hearts? Or perhaps John Lennon's words will become manifest; "for all the people who gain the world but lose themselves, they will see that we're all One and life flows on within you and without you." We must remember that balance is one of the key secrets of life. These transitional years ahead will certainly be wild. What this society, this country, this planet really needs is a return to balance, a respect for the miracle of creation, for nature, God, the family, the community, and each other. And by the Grace of God, one way or another, it *will* eventually happen, and we will be here to bear witness.

SuperConjunction 1994 promises an action-packed year and signals the two year warning. Two years until Pluto finishes 13 intensely Scorpionic years and enters fiery and inspirational Sagittarius. Two years until Uranus completes pulverizing and revolutionizing Capricornian structures and enters awakened Aquarius, the home sign of magic which it rules, and where it is at its best. Two years of Saturn completing Piscean karma before emerging into Aries to begin a fresh zodiacal cycle. We are like the mythological phoenix at the cusp of death and rebirth. For it is now just two years until the end of the two thousand year Piscean cycle, and the beginning of the true Aquarian Period, sign of the Water Bearer. Drink deeply of the Water of Life, my dear brothers and sisters.

To every time there is a season, and every season a purpose under the heavens

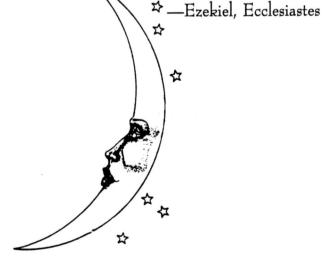

✩ —Ezekiel, Ecclesiastes

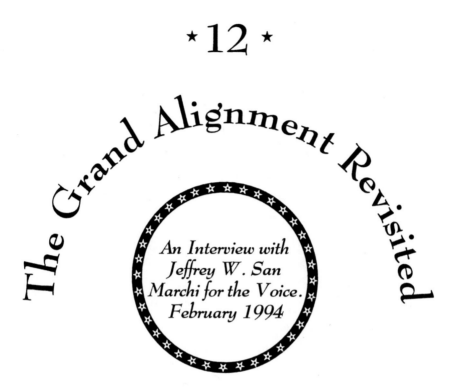

⋆ 12 ⋆

The Grand Alignment Revisited

An Interview with Jeffrey W. San Marchi for the Voice. February 1994

Editors Note:

While waiting to be reconnected to the electricity grid (like most folks in here in Ventura County on January 17th) I couldn't help but think about Ken Kalb's article published in the December 1993 Voice. Rereading it, a couple of key sentences popped out: "This New Year rocks & rolls here with the closest planetary alignment in several hundred years," and "I would say a *window of vulnerability* is definately wide open for Earth changes during the period of the Superconjunction." That gave me good enough reason to interview Ken and ask him some pertinent questions.

Jeffrey: Hey, Ken, gee whiz, you sure said something about an earthquake happening.

164

Ken: Well, I said it as creatively and gracefully as I could.

Jeffrey: Tell me about it.

Ken: Are you referring to what triggered my prognostications?

Jeffrey: Please!

Ken: Well Jeff, for over a 20 year period, I have observed the synchronicity of planetary alignments with increased terrestrial seismicity, volcanoes, and strange weather. During the time I was studying this major planetary alignment (which I dubbed *SuperConjunction 1994*), it triggered an intuitive response within me, both in recurring dreams, daydreams, and feelings that we were definately going to be getting some rocking and rolling. I kept seeing the freeways torn up and traffic endlessly gridlocked.

Jeffrey: Has anything like this ever happened for you before?

Ken: Yes, it has, but I've got to tell you, I am not in the business of predicting earthquakes—like the article I wrote for the *Voice*—the Earth change warning was not the prime focus. But I have had my share of precursor experiences. The first documented one was in June of 1976 when I was examining a very tight planetary alignment in Leo on the Eastern side of the chart, squared on both sides by Uranus and Jupiter. I kept getting the feeling that there was going to be a massive earthquake in China which I kept mentioning to several friends and associates. Then I wrote an article in June of 1976 with a very similar scenario—there would be a huge Earthquake on the *fire ring*, probably in China—on July 28th. To my own surprise and dismay, there was indeed a devastating trembler on that day in China which killed 675,000 people! I myself was astounded that this was correct.

Northridge Earthquake

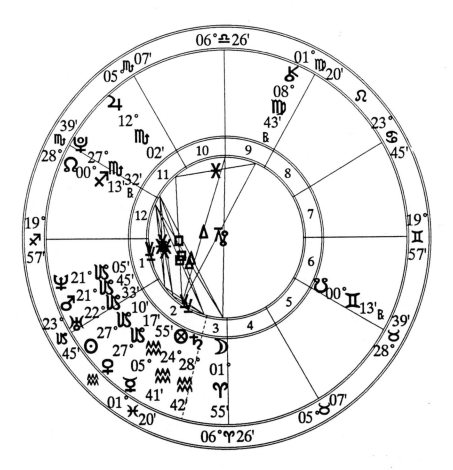

January 17, 1994
4:31 AM
Northridge, CA

The process is similar to doing an astrology reading. Studying the charts initiates a focusing process into the right issues and areas, and provides the format for timing. Once this information is digested, you're intuition springboards into visualizations of more specific scenarios. Another mind blowing circumstance occurred when Skip Lau and Charles DeWitt were at my home interviewing me for an upcoming TV show the next morning. I was explaining the concepts of sunspots and planetary alignments, and how we were entering another solar maximum with Saturn, Uranus, and Neptune aligned in Capricorn all opposing Jupiter. I was expressing thoughts about structures crumbling, like the Berlin Wall, but also how we were entering the *window for earth changes*, when suddenly my cottage started rocking and the phone rang, with a client calling to tell me to turn on the TV to see the *World Series* Loma Prieta earthquake. *Synchroni-city!* The gentleman looked at each other shaking their heads, and Skip exhorted, "just please be in the studio at 8 am tomorrow morning; We'll just fly on authomatic pilot on this one."

Jeffrey: Sunspots increase in a cycle?

Ken: Since Galileo first discovered sunspots in 1610, there have been a preponderance of sunspots every 11 years, increasing in amount roughly from year 9 to 11 in the cycle and back to year 9, before trailing back to normal. So it's approximately a 4 year window, but there are anomalies to this rule. The last solar maximum occured at the end of 1991 around the time of the eruption of Mt. Pinatubo.

Jeffrey: Can you explain the concept of planetary alignments, sunspots, and related phenomenon?

Ken: It's more of an astrophysics phenomenon than anything astrological, although there are correlatations both ways. There was a book written in 1974 by two Cambridge astrophysicists called *The Jupiter Effect*. Their research pointed to planetary alignments exacerbating solar activity, particularly during and around the 11-year sunspot maximum years. The book and the theory were fairly well debunked because the publishers engaged in distortions of their work due to crass sensationalization. But there are numerous other studies along the same lines like Joseph Goodavage's *Our Threatened Planet*, the work of astrometeorologist George J. McCormick, or the RCA studies by Dr. John Nelson, among hundreds of others which validate the connections between these same influences in less adulterated form. I wrote an article in 1982 called *The Grand Planetary Alignment* to try to separate the wheat from the chaff as far as what was right and wrong with *The Jupiter Effect* because the book was causing an international stir. I found that the publisher sensationalized the theory by making the alignment look like pearls on a string, rather than staggered in a 95 degree arc in space—and by making certain sensationalist statements like "the San Andreas fault will be subjected to the most massive earthquake known in the populated regions of earth in this century." They apparently slipped that kind of thing in to stimulate the fear level and sell more copies of the book. Due to this, most scientists reacted rather fiercely against their work, resulting in tossing the proberbial baby out with the bath water.

Jeffrey: Are you saying that the scientists were misquoted by their publishers?

Ken: It certainly appears that way. It looks as though they were both misquoted and the publisher added statements that the scientists didn't even make. And the cover of the book is a dead giveaway: It depicts the planets as though they're on a straight plumb line to the Sun; and uses the fearsome subtitle, *The planets as triggers of devastating earthquakes.*

But remember, here were two top Cambridge astrophysicists predicting the big earthquake. This wasn't *Criswell Predicts* or some Ramtha or Mafu channeling, or even a revived Nostradamus prediction. Here were two highly respected and supposedly credible members of the scientific establishment basing their work on volumes of solid research published under the *science* category, predicting the long overdue *Big One.*

Jeffrey: So where's the beef, or maybe I should say tofu of the theory?

Ken: The valid part of the theory, as I see it, is essentially that the planets do affect solar tides and increase the solar wind as they orbit the Sun, similar to the way the moon creates tides on the Earth. The difference is that the Sun is composed of multi-million degree helium and exploding gases. Even though the planets are far away, they exert enough gravitational and electromagnetic force to stimulate and accelerate solar activity, particularly when they align or interact with sunspots. Remember, the great scientist Sir Isaac Newton discovered gravity when an apple fell off a tree, and scientists have been very diffuse and obtuse in explaining just what or why gravity really is since then. Solar activity comes in the form of solar flares, prominences, sunspots, coronal holes and an increase in the solar wind. Possibly the alignments pierce holes in the surface of the sun called coronal holes. Out of these gusts the solar wind which is a constant gale of atomic particles spiraling out of the sun's magnetic field, ejecting into space some 3000 tons or so of mass each hour at from one to two million miles per hour!

169

Chinese Earthquake

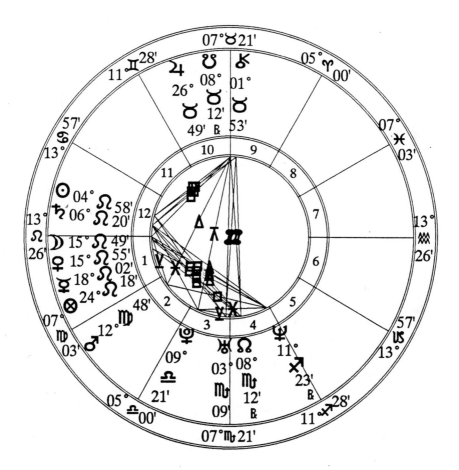

July 28, 1976
6:00 AM
T'ang-shan, NE China

Now I am not an astrophysicist. But by watching the dovetailing periods of sunspot activity and planetary alignments, and intuitively dialing in, I've been able to forwarn in published works prior to several incidents of heightened earth change activity (I call a ripe time a *window of vulnerability*), though it was a sidelight—not the specific focus of my writings. So I think this phenomena is something that geologists, astrophysicists, and other interested people should examine very carefully for the future.

From most of my own research and the studies I've analyzed, astronomical oppositions and conjunctions, and (possibly also the squares) all seem to work similarly. I believe they have a gravitational and/or electromagnetic influence which exacerbates the occurrence of activity on the Sun—meaning solar flares, prominences, sunspots, and coronal holes—which blast atomic particles out into space where they get caught in our Earth's atmosphere, in turn slowing the earth's rotation down a bit which increases the stress on the tectonic plate margins, thus increasing the possibility of earthquakes, volcanoes, strange weather and the like. But it's critical to mention that there doesn't have to be an alignment or a sunspot peak to have earthquakes. There are many unseen forces constantly at work which are on nature's agenda. For example, there are several scientists who postulate we're currently in the downpour of a meteor shower.

Jeffrey: Were there alot of sunspots at the time of the Northridge quake?

Ken: I called the Solar Terrestrial Physics division of the National Geophysical Data Center in Colorado and asked them for the sunspot numbers for January. They were no higher than normal. So I asked if there was any other unusual solar phenomenon on record. Sure enough, they found that there was *tremendously enhanced geomagnetic activity* from the coronal holes which increased on the 16th to about *triple* their normal levels which began decreasing around the 20th or 21st of January back to normal. I'm not saying this is a solid proof, but it is another good indication that there is a connection between solar activity, planetary alignments, and earthquakes which should be examined by professionals.

Jeffrey: Have you looked ahead for other alignments and *windows of vulnerability?*

Ken: Yes. In early May of 2000, there is a very tight alignment of seven planets in conjunction with the other two planets squaring the seven. This alignment occurs right at the peak of the next sunspot maximum. One other powerful feature of this line-up is that massive Jupiter sits right in the center of it. There are also some other strong alignments before that—in December of 1995 and January of 1996, for example. Physicist John Zajak claims that earthquake activity is highly accelerated at this time—that we're having 6000 percent more earthquakes now than 40 years ago. There is no doubt that we are in a stimulated period of cataclysms; I'm particularly concerned about Japan, and the ramifications that a severe earthquake there would have not only on people's lives, but also on the entire global banking and economic system. So I think the astrophysicists and geologists at CalTech and other earthquake research centers should be examining and monitoring solar activity and these related dynamics as a possible warning mechanism for earth changes and be getting the message to the Japanese and others. Then again, as Bob Dylan once sang "you don't have to be a weatherman to know which way the wind blows," so you may just wish to tune into your own feelings and conclusions, and take appropriate actiion. Twenty five years ago when I looked at this May of 2000 alignment and considered that this may be the a year of major Earth changes, it seemed like a comfortably long time away. But now it's just a couple of twists and turns down the road. It brings up a whole range of issues centered around preparedness and readiness for earthquakes. My feeling is that Southern Californians should act like the *Big One* is going to come on December 31st of 1994, and get seriously busy making the necessary preparations and changes for it. The San Andreas fault, the border of the Pacific and North American tectonic plates last released way back in 1857—137 years ago, and averages a big slip every 131 years, so it's on overtime, with scientists saying it would produce a quake in the 8's. But the entire L.A. area alone is riddled with overdue faults, like the Newport-Inglewood fault running through Santa Monica and W.L.A. And there have now been three powerful warnings.

Jeffrey: What key issues does this bring up?

Ken: Several things need to be looked at right between the eyes. Anyone living in Southern California needs to ask themselves; Do you really want to be here? Sure, virtually every area has its pitfalls: Florida has its hurricanes, the Midwest has its tornadoes, the East its bitter cold. And Southern California has its earthquakes, fires, air pollution and floods. So three key questions must be addressed: Where do you want to be? Who do you want to be with? And, what do you want to do? If the answer is not in Southern California or you have another option, you should consider leaving soon. But if you do want to stake your claim there, then it is time to get busy making some big changes. Human nature has proven that it rarely makes plans out of awareness. We hardly even respond to emergencies. It usually takes catastrophe to trigger action. Then, shortly thereafter, people get amnesia within the apparent stability of nature! So with a major catastrophe looming, before the dust settles and the Earth revolts again, we should all take inventory on what can be done to prepare for the future and do it!

Solar activity needs to be seriously monitored and examined by researchers. The problem with *The Jupiter Effect* was not the basic theory. Alot of good research ended up washing down the drain because the publishers of the book got greedy and sensationalized a theory that probably does have a lot of validity. It has simply happened too many times in my short life where I have seen earthquakes, volcanoes, and strange weather in synchronicity with planetary alignments and/or sunspot maximums. Right at the last sunspot peak, Mt. Pinatubo erupted furiously, the Mississippi river flooded like it never has before, Hurricane Iniki devastated Kauai, among much other heightened activity. I hope some aspiring scientist reading these words might just want to take the bull by the horns and thrust some fresh energy into this project. It may just end up saving a couple of million lives!

Jeffrey: So what can we do?

Ken: This catastrophe is a wake up call. Reeling in wreckage on shaky ground with no water, power, or information is vulnerability-city! Everyone needs to pay critical attention to all of the earthquake preparedness information which will be coming down the line, and take action on it. And in 3, 6, or 9 months don't get amnesia and become complacent, because right when you start to forget, another very rude awakening may come which could really put you to sleep!

But this signals the need for bolder changes, like getting off the electric grid and phasing into energy self sufficiency. This lifestyle of one-person, one-car traveling in a polluting machine for long distances to work and play needs to be changed. The sight of a hundred thousand spectators driving to see an athletic event in an arena sitting on a huge fault under nuclear powered lights is pretty ludicrous. Get your legs in shape and start walking; get your bike in tune and start riding. Get on the metrolink. There is absolutely no reason why Southern California with its abundance of sunshine cannot live on solar energy! Fifteen years ago, California had a 55 percent tax credit for solar energy installations. It's zero now. We need to restore, even amplify this policy. We truly need to take a Manhattan project mentality toward alternative energy, and get it in place as soon as we can. Mayor Riordan and the city council should make rapid transit a top priority. The *defense conversion* the Clinton administration proselytized during the campaign should focus squarely in this direction. Defense contractors should shift gears right now into becoming renewable energy producers and be awarded government contracts. This would address both our air pollution and defense-conversion employment problems simultaneously. Our broken up freeways are testimony to the absurdity of trucking food and fuel hundreds of miles to the marketplace. Food should be grown locally and near distribution centers. Earthquake-proof emergency water storage containers should be built. We can live without power, but not without water!

We can live without power, but not without water!

Electric car technology should be government subsidized and accelerated into the marketplace faster than the current timetable of mandates. Our building codes need to be reviewed and revised to require structures to withstand earthquakes in the 8.5, maybe even 9.0 range, even if it's not cost effective. Schools at all levels should implement mandatory classes in earthquake preparedness, besides accelerated earthquake drills for students. Our downscaling military should be trained to deal with and assist in local catastrophes, rather than skirmishes abroad. This is also a time to starting thinking more in terms of community, so get to know your neighbors, and their neighbors as well: In the face of cataclysm, we're *all* family. Mother Nature has her own cycles and agenda for change, and we must learn to adapt and live by them, rather than live in the hypnosis of her apparent stability. The time has come for big changes, or else the next time she sneezes, burps, or farts we might just find ourselves trapped in a world with nowhere to run or hide. We have the resources, the know-how, and the need to ride out the coming cataclysms; & we have just been harshly warned by Mother Nature to get busy *right now* creating a better world.

Jeffrey: Is there any Silver Lining for Southern California in this disaster?

Ken: There actually is. Southern California's architects and civil engineers are designing some of the strongest structures in modern civilization. I was on the 14th floor of a high rise during a 6.5 two years ago built on a *ball*, and the building rode it out very well without any damage. It sure flipped my wig though! New structures in this area are being built to very strict codes, and people here are also more psychologically prepared now for these kinds of events than in other areas of the world. A fault map of the U.S. or world shows that the entire planet looks like an egg that has been dropped. Other areas are nowhere near as ready both structurally or psychologically, so in this way California may have the cataclysm advantage. This Earth is very much alive and going through lots of changes as the human species treats her delicate balances with the severe brutality of a civilization growing rampantly. We live in Mother Nature's womb which provides all the nourishment we need to support our lives. We must reciprocate this tenderness with which we are being nurtured with these gifts. Just imagine a baby living inside his mother—smoking, trashing, excavating, developing, polluting & poisoning his loving support system. But that's somewhat analagous to our life on Earth. We need to get the golden rule shining brightly through our relationship with life once again.

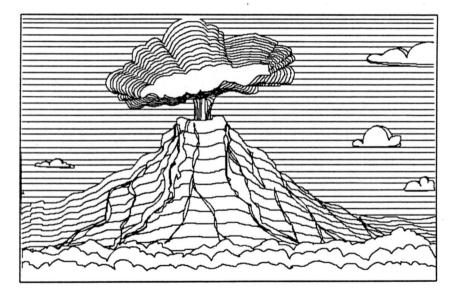

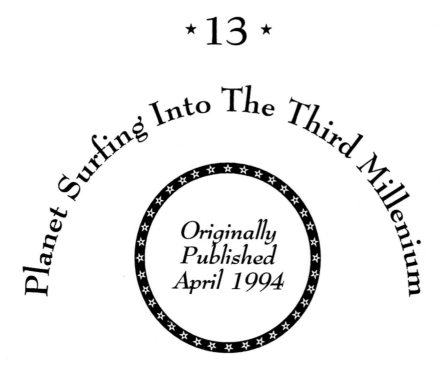

★ 13 ★

Planet Surfing Into The Third Millenium

Originally
Published
April 1994

The Magic of Surfing

What is it about the activity of riding waves which makes it so joyously addictive? The *Surfer General* has warned that surfing is twice as addictive as sex, five times as pleasurable as marijuana, and ten times healthier than both put together. Back in the older days of surfing when we had to learn on thirty pound longboards, the learning curve was as steep as a critical takeoff at Rincon. But without wetsuits or leashes, or sometimes even rides to the beach, we braved the elements and paid major dues to learn this sacred *sport of Kings. Catch a wave and your sittin' on top of the world*, harmonized the Beach Boys in the 60's. And there was alot of truth in that line, for when every surfer gets that first real ride they're pretty well hooked. Why? Because surfing is just plain *Cosmic!* Think about it. Just for there to be intelligent and enjoyable life on a planet in this Universe is an amazing one in many million phenomena in itself. Carl Sagan could tell you just how many millions and millions and millions those odds are. But for there to be a planet with all these beautiful places with perfectly formed waves, and beings who have developed finely tuned crafts to gracefully dance on these waves is simply *Magical!* Then there is the full-on nature trip; the elemental aspect of playing in the primordial broth from which life itself sprang. To be totally immersed in the purity and freedom of nature's life force amidst the water and the sun, the wind or the rain is thoroughly refreshing and invigorating. Every surfer can certainly thank his Lucky Stars!

But for there to be a planet with all these beautiful places with perfectly formed waves, and beings who have developed finely tuned crafts to gracefully dance on these waves is simply Magical!

A friend of mine insists this *surf addiction* or craze is simply from some type of archetypal emulation of Jesus walking on the water. I don't know? Maybe it's just the challenge. Or, perhaps it boils down to that divinely sensual *feeling* you get, or like the dolphins and the Chumash, the sheer freedom and joy. All I know is that smoothly carving the face of a glassy wave, sun caressing my back, the only way to relate the feeling in my heart is to say it's like.... *making love with God.*

SURFING USA 1994

Whatever it is, surfing has caught fire. It created a lifestyle, spawned a subculture, and engendered an industry. From surf shops to surf music to surf clothes to surf wagons, surf culture has spread infectiously. From surf movies to surf museums to surf bars to surf contests to surf camps to Prime Ticket covering 42 hours of surf programming going into over 41 million homes this year, surfing has evolved from clique to global pheonomena. Surfer magazine, who turns thirty five this year, said there were about 3000 active surfers in 1960 in the U.S. Now there are 1.5 million. When surf fashions peaked in the 80's, they were wearing hooded flannel shirts from Kansas to Korea. This year, Americans will buy 315,000 surfboards, 162,000 snowboards, 450,000 volleyballs and 467,500 wetsuits, and will spend $405 million on clothes to wear while using this equipment. Add the figures for boogie boards, knee boards, skate boards, windsurfing equipment, surf kayaks, jet skis, all the associated paraphenalia, sport utility vehicles, travel and expenses, and you approach the gross national product of a small third world country, or even a couple of days interest on our national debt! And after *Endless Summer II* hits the silver screen this summer thirty years after the original, we could see another boost which radically alters the surfing landscape into new dimensions of popularity.

THE UNPREDICTABLE ADVENTURE

Virtually every surfer on the planet has figured out how to punctuate his existence to be in sufficient control of his time to be able to surf when it's good. And most, to a greater or lesser extent, have designed their lives around their surfing. Some would argue that surfing retards professional development or career advancement. Most surfers would counter that it was well worth it. Like the art of wave riding itself, most surfers have devised a balance between their responsibilities and their freedom to surf. For surfing is like life itself; its all about timing & balance: And, *staying stoked.*

Unlike most activities, surfing is totally weather dependent and therefore tricky to plan the when and where of it. Like riding a wave, you must be in the right place at the right time. Its about interconnectedness: The Sun, the Earth, the Moon, the tides, the wind, the rain, the swell direction. From aligning with the *Big Kahuna,* to understanding planetary alignments, sunspots, weather patterns, buoy reports, surf faxes and hotlines; knowing when and where it's good. Being there and doing it. That's what it's all about.

Ten Major Innovations Which Have Revolutionized Surfing
1960 -1994

1. The Foam and Fiberglass surfboard
2. The Short board
3. The Surf leash
4. The Twin Fin
5. The Thruster
6. The Surfing Wetsuit
7. Surf Wax & Traction Material
8. HiTech Materials, Computer Design, Shaping Machines
9. The Boogie Board
10. The Modern Longboard

THE COMEBACK KID: THE LONGBOARD

Ten years or so ago, not too many surfers would have thought that it would have been the *Modern Longboard* which would be the hottest ticket in the surf shop. I can remember even just a *few* years ago being discriminated against as a "f_____g longboarder," as I would glide into wave after wave at the Point. But it's back, and like Rock N' Roll, it's here to stay. Unlike its predecessors, this longboard is a different breed; a lean, mean, high performance machine. Fourteen pounds of beautiful sculpture, capable of carving the face of a critical wave, or walking the nose in weak summertime junk; the modern longboard represents a synthesis of 30 years of surfing evolution, and we're stoked!

THE CHALLENGE TO SURFING: ENVIRONMENTAL POLLUTION AND CROWDS

In these last half dozen years of this last decade of the final century before the Third Millenium, population and progress has had the side effect of making Mother Earth ill. Her fragile and balanced ecosystems are being terribly challenged. The oceans are polluted, the seas and forests are dying. Our tropical rain forests, the lungs of the planet, are being cut down at a rate which could see them disappear by the turn of the century! The waste gas from industry, automobiles, the military, government, and households are destabilizing the atmopshere, and many scientists believe the planet is warming and the ozone layer depleting to near cataclysmic levels. Seventy percent of this planet's surface is ocean with an average depth of 3800 feet. In this cradle of evolution dwell the planet's only stable communities, species little changed in hundreds of millions of years; including the crown of creation, the whales and dolphins. But Mother Nature is so resilient that she can absorb this tremendous impact of man.....up to a point, *which we have **now** reached.*

KenKalb at Rincon, Santa Barbara

Here in California we live on the Western edge of our continent. Our beautiful beaches are both our playgrounds and the barometers of this environmental challenge. Southern California has lost 1400 beaches in the last few decades. With the postwar population explosion, urbanization, booming industrialization, and poor environmental planning, our beaches have become increasingly poisoned. To love is to care, so beach lovers should share in trying to turn the tide on this degradation of our coastline and the ocean. The best form of teaching is by demonstration; so each of us who learns and lives a low-environmental impact lifestyle radiates an example for others to follow. Mother Earth is a womb, not a tomb.

THE SURFRIDER FOUNDATION: FACING THE MUSIC WITH ACTION

Ventura County has one of the strongest local chapters of the ten year old environmental and educational organization known as the *Surfrider Foundation*. With about 30 core and 600 peripheral members, *Surfrider* engages in a variety of activities to help preserve the quality of our beaches and raise public environmental consciousness. Beach cleanups, water testing, storm drain stenciling, beach access, burning beachfront issues, and preserving the integrity of the coastline are some of the focal points of their activity. *Glen Kent* of Ventura *Surfrider* is optimistic because he feels that "people's habits are slowly changing," and it is "becoming culturally unacceptable to degrade the environment." He feels that most people are aware there is a problem and want to help so one principle task is to "help people get to know the right things to do, like how to dispose of things properly." "We need to simply remember that everything washes down to the rivers, and the rivers wash down to the oceans." That which goes down a storm drain, like whatever you hose off your driveway, from antifreeze to doggie poop goes through the sewers and into the oceans." *Surfrider* and the city are currently cooperating in a storm drain stenciling program, where volunteers mark drains with the warning, "this storm drain leads to the ocean." People need to be aware of the entire cycle of disposal, think about the consequences of their actions, and take responsibility for them. While the EPA is getting stricter with environmental laws, private, public and governmental awareness and action must continue rising to the challenges of our post industrial society, if we are to create a beach loving future. By the way, support the *Surfrider Foundation*: Buy a T-shirt, join in a beach cleanup, donate some tax-deductible money, or join. Their national phone number is 1-800-743-SURF. The table below, courtesy of *Surfrider's Blue Water Task Force* water testing, finds that some of our favorite beaches and surfspots are becoming akin to swimming or surfing in a toilet! And this is just the amount of ecoliform bacteria from urban runoff, and doesn't include oil spills, pesticides, and other hazardous materials.

Surfrider Foundation Ocean Sampling Bacteria Report

Week Of:	3/6/94	2/27/94	2/20/94	2/13/94	2/6/94	1/30/94
Rincon	4	2	2	0	n/a	1
Stables	n/a	3	5	4	2	0
South Jetty	1	1	3	1	5	1
Surfer's Knoll	5	2	5	3	5	1
McGrath	2	2	3	1	5	1
Gonzales Rd.	1	1	5	1	3	1
Mandalay Edison	1	1	n/a	1	5	1
Silver Strand	0	0	0	n/a	n/a	0
LA County line	Volunteer needed for County Line					

Rating Chart of Coliform Bacteria Amounts

0- None Detected

1 - Below Shellfish Standard (Generally considered safe to munch on shellfish harvested from this water

2 - Above Shellfish Standard (Generally considered unsafe for shellfish harvesting for human consumption)

3 - Near Body Contact Standard (Caution advised for prolonged surfing, swimming, floundering or shredding)

4 - Above Body Contact Standard (Body contact not advised. Sore throat, sinus, ear)

5 - Very High Counts (Unsafe. Polluted, yucky, heinous. Stay Out!)

Pretty scary stuff! Myself and lots of surfers have gotten very sick and a few have even died from pollution. And what about our children, and our children's children? The sad reality that man is poisoning the sacred sea is truly profane. Can we turn this ever-reddening tide around?

CROWDS: THE SOLUTION IS R-E-S-P-E-C-T

By the laws of arithmetic, if you divide more surfers into less surf spots you get crowds. With higher flotation surfboards catching more waves, occasionally the lineup turns into what surfer's call a *zoo*. When the testoserone levels are running high in the water, any number of bizarre, even violent scenarios can go off from bad vibes to fights which detract from the magic of surfing. Surfing is one of the only totally unregulated sports, and few surfer's would like to see rules and enforcement. So the only solution is **mutual respect**. We must all try to share waves, keep the peace, and try to enjoy our brother and sister surfers getting a ride (almost)as much as ourselves. Then again, perhaps after *Endless Summer II*, *Big Wednesday III*, Disney's rumored *Dewey Weber* movie, a resurgence in popularity might get venture capitalists to start building more *Surfatoriums* with wave machines producing perfect waves which will thin out crowds. Not quite the same thing, eh? Well, possibly the government will allow the production of computer designed surf spots with perfect artificial reefs made from recycled materials producing a triple winner: Safe waste disposal, fish spawning areas, and *new surfspots*! Otherwise, by the turn of the century we may just see a science fiction scenario like the nightmare described below.

C STREET 2000: A SCI-FI NIGHTMARE

All surfer's must take a test to procure their surfing license. If you pass both your written water safety and proficiency exams, you will only be able to surf during designated hours based on which color surf pass you purchase to display on your board, from the high priced *unlimited* to the budget *off hours*. Helmeted armed lifeguards will patrol the lineup on red 12' boards and jet skis enforcing both the hours and any infractions of the *Surfing Code*. Surfer's may receive tickets for such violations as snaking, paddling out through the lineup, pulling leashes, kicking out on someone, violence, or even the dreaded SUI (surfing under the influence). Penalties will range from simple removal from the water for the day, to suspensions, fines, all-day attendance at an inland surfing school, or jail time. *Are we still having any fun?* **No way!**

So to avoid this sort of a dreadful scenario, all us surfers will need to practice some behavioral modification as crowds increase, to become more dolphinlike in the water; friendly, respectful, and joyous. And of course, there is another solution: Travel.

THE ENDLESS SUMMER: TRAVEL TIME

Paul Nielsen, owner of *Waveline*, the good-vibe surf shop at the point, is pretty locked into his activities as a surfer, surf-dad, surf shop owner, NSSA competition director, and *Surfrider* supporter. But whenever he can, he travels to exotic paradises to surf pristine waters and uncrowded waves. Paul really lights it up when he starts talking about the thousands of places all over this planet that are now accessible by boat or jet plane compared to the old days. "Travel is the big bonus of being a surfer," exclaims Nielsen. He's looking forward to the day when he co-owns his shop with his son who will send him an occasional check to *"General Delivery, Paradise,"* so he can focus on fully blissing out in various exotic global surf heavens.

Ken Kalb at Miramar, Santa Barbara

FOR THE LOVE OF THE SPORT

David Puu, ex-surfing champion and owner of *MorningStar Surf and Sport* is a Ventura resident who has dedicated his life to all aspects of surfing. Surfing, shaping, glassing, sanding, creating new designs, competing, coaching, marketing; this man lives all aspects of the surfing lifestyle. You wouldn't see this kind of dedication in any other sport; for example, no tennis fanatic would be designing racquets, balls, courts, playing tournaments, selling equipment, and coaching, would you? Incidentally, David broadcasts one of the finest surf reports I have ever heard. "It's simply all about Love," says David. After competing for years, in scores of events all over the world, David feels that the best competitive surfers are the ones who truly love the sport, not the ego-trippers or dollar chasers. "Surfing is unique because it is a lifetime sport which combines wave knowledge, athletic skill, and a level of dedication which transforms it into a lifestyle," says Puu. After reviewing the skimpy economic rewards reaped by everyone in the surfing industry, David feels everyone involved with surfing is simply there....... *"for the love of the sport."* David and I finished our conversation on a philosphical note:

Ken: "I'll probably surf until I die, or die surfing."
Dave: "Yeah, either way's just fine."
Ken: "And then we can ride tandem on the cosmic wave with the *Big Kahuna*."
Dave: "Yeah, I'm stoked!"

Ken Kalb, the author.

★ 14 ★

Great Balls of Cosmic Fire

Originally Published July 1994

ifteen billion years after the cataclysm which formed our solar system, planet Earth has evolved a conscious species with a technologically advanced civilization about to experience another cosmic cataclysm.

From July 16 at around 11:30 pm pdt, to July 22, 1994, a convoy of 22 comet fragments, interplanetary vagabonds from deep space traveling at 133,000 miles per hour will complete their celestial collision course and crash into Jupiter. The major fragments which range from about 1/2 to 2 1/2 miles in diameter are expected to create an explosion releasing the equivalent of 500 million tons of TNT, or more energy than all of the nuclear devices ever exploded on Earth. Twelve days after millions of Americans on Earth blow off their sparklers, God has planned a little fireworks of His own, with giant Jupiter expected to glow in twice its normal brilliance. And nobody knows what's really going to happen.

For 5 1/2 days at least, Earthlings will have something miraculous to take their minds off of the O.J. Simpson trial. Scientists will feast on a cornucopia of fresh astronomic delights to digest. And Earthlings will witness a reminder of the fragility of existence as we watch something which could happen to our own planet that could take us out in a flash.

65 million years ago it is postulated that a similar cosmic collision occured here on Earth which among other effects, extinguished all the sturdy dinosaurs who had been thriving for a hundred million years. When this theoretical comet or asteroid nailed our Earth, it raised a dust cloud which blocked the sunlight and killed the photosynthesizing plant life which was the main food source of the dinosaurs, who in turn perished shortly thereafter. Modern man who has been here only one thousandth this much time, has been so busy destroying the planet and his fellow man in pursuit of money, that the odds for self destruction are much greater than those of any such cosmic annihilation.

But on March 31, 1989 a 1/2 mile wide asteroid or comet whizzed through the Earth's orbit, flying through the position the Earth occupied just six hours earlier—about 1/2 million miles away. Scientists testifying about this before the House of Representatives claimed this "would have caused a disaster unprecedented in human history." Two other close flybys were discovered in 1989, 6 in 1990, and the closest one yet (125,000 miles) in 1993. The odds of such a catastrophe are not as farfetched as one might think, claims Clark Chapman of the Planetary Science Institute in Tucson Arizona. In the January issue of Nature he claimed that the odds of a comet plastering the Earth in your lifetime are about one in 20,000; about the same as dying in an airplane crash or major flood. Chapman says its not a question of whether we'll sustain a large impact, it's a matter of when.

I think its pretty wild that in the 4 billion years of Earth's existence this is happening right when modern man has developed advanced observation and diagnostic devices, and even has the Galileo space probe and Hubble telescope in position to transmit and photograph this spectacular event! It is also quite miraculous that someone was able to spot these travelers, let alone track and predict exactly when and where they are going to make their impact. With all deference to the discoverer's, I just wish they would give such a magnificent and rare event a better name than Shoemaker-Levy 9.

Another absolutely uncanny coincidence is that comet week is precisely synchronous with the 25th anniversary of Moon week in 1969; with the launch of the Saturn 5 rocket which transported Neil Armstrong and the Apollo 11 crew departing on July 16th, landing on the 20th and returning on the 22nd.

Though the comets are shooting for landings on the far side of Jupiter, Galileo will have a direct view, and because of Jupiter's rapid rotation each explosive impact should swing into telescopic sight within the hour to transmit back to us here on Earth.

Just imagine for a moment sitting on the beach when suddenly a giant 747 comes crashing down from the sky into the ocean. Wow! Now imagine if you can, a fleet of 22 of these 747's, except—they're a hundred to five hundred times bigger and they're going 500 times faster—colliding into the ocean. That's sort of what's happening up there on Jupiter.

The range of physical effects speculated to result from the comet collisions are vast:

1. Unleash mushroom clouds, plumes, & fireballs up to 2000 miles into the Jovian atmosphere creating a series of brilliant SuperNova-like flashes.

2. Explode into a meteor shower as the comets flash and sparkle brilliantly upon entry into the Jovian atmopshere where they create huge Earth-size Jupiter quakes.

3. Thicken Jupiter's thin ring into something akin to Saturn's magnificent bands as the dust and debris park in orbit—right before our very eyes.

4. Create a second red spot giving the cycloptic Jupiter a second or even third eye.

5. Knock Jupiter slightly out of its orbit creating an oscillation across the surface of Jupiter which may be felt subtly throughout the entire solar system.

6. Disturb Jupiter's magnetic field which in turn exacerbates solar activity such as sunspots, flares, coronal holes and the solar wind which in turn effects terrestrial weather, seismicity, and consciousness.

7. Make a little thud and a big dud as the icy nuclei of the comets melt during the heat of entry, with the remaining mass splashing softly into the deep cloud tops of the Jovian atmosphere.

No matter what happens, all eyes will be on Jupiter during comet week 1994 with virtually every telescope on Earth and even an airborne observatory in place to observe and record the phenomenon. This will be the week when all of us will *get struck* by this comet. So lets get to know just who and what we're looking at.

A "CRASH COURSE" ON JUPITER

483 million miles from our Sun circles the fifth planet Jupiter, the King of planets. 1300 times bigger than our Earth and over twice as massive as all the other planets combined, it is like a miniature solar system with its 16 moons. The four inner moons, Europa, Io, Callisto, and Ganymede were discovered by Galileo in 1610 and are around the size of Earth's Moon. The others are smaller with the outer 4 spinning retrograde to Jupiter's motion. Scientists say if Jupiter were just several times larger, its internal pressures would have created the nuclear fusion reaction in its hydrogen and helium mass to make it a star. Jupiter takes almost twelve years (11.86) to complete an orbit, but rotates so fast that its *day* is just under 10 hours. The energy in its magnetic field (magnetosphere) extends out 10 times Jupiter's diameter and is 4000 times larger than the Earth's. It is the only planet which generates its own light rather than reflecting the Sun's, so from deep space our solar system probably appears to have a binary or double star.

Jupiter is a *soft* planet. Like the Sun and primeval nebula, Jupiter is mostly composed of hydrogen and helium. It has no solid surface, only a gradual transition from gas to liquid to a point about a quarter of the way into the planet which

195

Carl Sagan

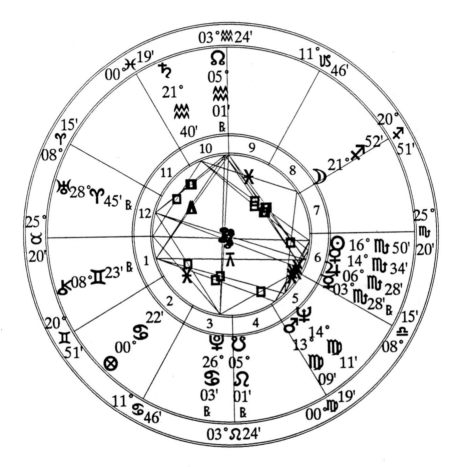

November 9, 1934
5:05 PM
Brooklyn, NY

becomes metallic and somewhat solid. Astronomers think the planet has three layers of crystalline clouds, each separated by about 20 miles, which appear in psychedelic swirls of blue, brown, orange, white and red. Storms and giant eddies form and dissipate, with some like the Earth-size giant red spot perpetuating for thousands, even hundreds of thousands of years.

THE MYTHOLOGY OF JUPITER

In Roman mythology, Jupiter was known as Jove, the king of the gods, ruler of the pantheon, and lord of life and death. Jupiter, which means *shining father* in Latin, was the son of Saturn and Rhea, the husband of Juno, and the father of Minerva, Apollo, and Hercules among a long line of other gods and goddesses. The Romans identified him with the Greek god Zeus, though he differed in certain respects such as never visiting humans on earth. Mythological Jupiter was a sky god equipped with a sheaf of thunderbolts which he could fire down to Earth to administer his intense and creative forms of justice. The links between the astrological influence of Jupiter and its mythological namesake, however, are not as solid as is the case with many other planets.

THE IMPACT ON OUR INNER SPACE

Will this event have a spiritual or metaphysical significance beyond the material physics of the phenomenon? If the landing happened 500 years ago before our advanced telescopes and computers warned us, would our

O.J. Simpson

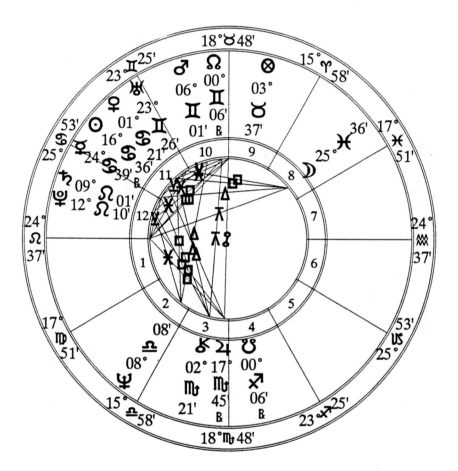

July 9, 1947
8:08 AM
San Francisco, CA

lives still be impacted? For those who take a holistic view of the universe, and feel the interconnectedness of all things including our solar system, the answer is yes indeed. We know there will be hundreds of millions, perhaps even billions of eyes trained on Jupiter. What will our inner eye see and what will we feel? So let's meditate on who Jupiter is in the metaphysical dimension.

Jupiter is the King of planets. His domain is the order of creation. In our lives, Jupiter is the light on our paths toward true selfhood and our life purpose. So perhaps the impact will scramble this order like a cue ball breaking the pack to start our new *game*. The impact will likely cause a jolt or *kick in our paths*; a cosmic alarm clock sounding its wake up call for a course correction, new direction, activation, or leap in our lives. Sometimes growth spurts have their pain or squeeze out some negativity as well, but ultimately turn out positive. Have there been any thunderbolts in your life lately? There have been in mine!

Jupiter, ruler of Sagittarius represents the illumination of the intellect by the light of the spirit. A light capable of transforming the time-space function of the human mind into the awakened christ consciousness of truth and love.

Jupiter, ruler of Sagittarius represents the illumination of the intellect by the light of the spirit. A light capable of transforming the time-space function of the human mind into the awakened christ consciousness of truth and love. Thus

Initial Comet Impact 'A'

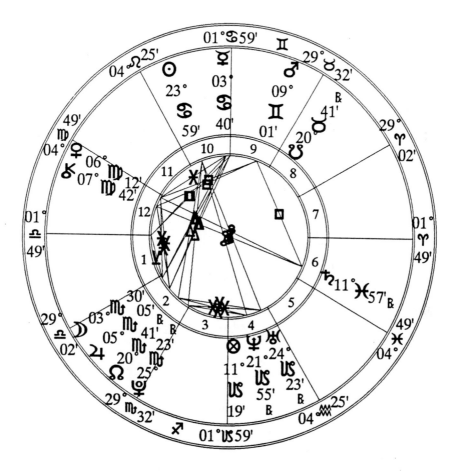

July 16, 1994
11:30 AM
Santa Barbara, CA

illuminated it is that part within us that intuitively knows our way, our divine wisdom or higher self. So perhaps the intense heat, light, and sound released by the comets will be synchronous with internal illuminations, intensified feelings, and awakened messages in our own lives. Since Jupiter rules religion and spirituality, perhaps the penetration of the Jovian environment with fresh light and energy from outer space will help shatter some of the anthropomorphic dogmas and divisions toward one of true universal love.

So perhaps the impact will scramble this order like a cue ball breaking the pack to start our new game. The impact will likely cause a jolt or kick in our paths; a cosmic alarm clock sounding its wake up call for a course correction, new direction, activation, or leap in our lives.

COMET CRASH ASTROLOGY

Jupiter is known as the *greater benefic* in astrology; the planet of expansion, optimism, opportunity, good fortune, prosperity, generosity, wealth, and success. It is also the planet of wisdom, philosophy, and justice. Much of this wisdom comes from what is experienced during adventures and explorations of various sorts. Jupiter is also the planet of angels, benevolence and luck. It brings assistance when you go to sleep at night so you awaken in the morning with resoluton and fresh clarity. And there certainly has been a major increase in the amount of interest and talk about angels—

Galileo Galilei

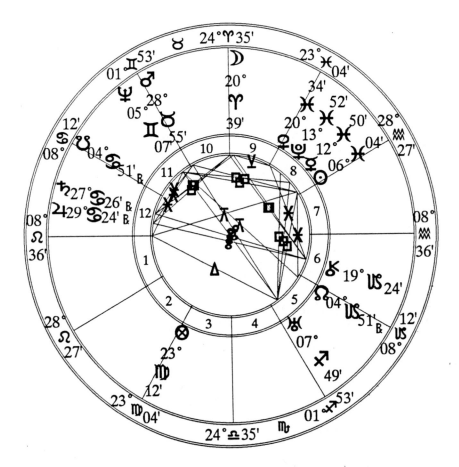

February 15, 1564
2:32:11 PM
Pisa, Italy

even in the mainstream media—in synchronicity with the comet phenomenon; its breakup two years ago which caused its radiance which led to its discovery and now its current approach and collision.

But do not fear this cataclysm; I believe that almost anything involving Jupiter will ultimately turn out for the good.

THE INITIAL IMPACT CHART

The tightest and most powerful aspect of the chart is an opposition between the Sun in Cancer and Uranus in Capricorn during the first impact; perfect for full awareness of the unusual and unpredictable which may challenge and awaken our personal identities. There is absolutely no fire in the chart, with 6 planets in water, 3 in Earth and one in Air; an emotional chart with alot happening on the inner planes. There is a a T-square between Mars, Venus and Chiron, and Saturn, and a Mystic Rectangle between the Sun, Pluto, the South Node and Uranus and Neptune, with soft aspects outnumbering hard aspects 2 to 1. This suggests a period of internal dynamism with a mellow and positive outcome. The Moon makes its monthly conjunction to Jupiter shortly after impact, a time of strong optimism even in Scorpio, and enters its second quarter phase reaching full Moon right around the final impact. Venus and Chiron are conjunct in Virgo with both sextiling the Moon and Jupiter, indicating that silver threads and golden needles are weaving their healing energy on our emotional bodies. There is a balance between the cardinal, fixed, and mutable modes in the chart. Mercury has been out of its retrograde for ten days now and is

PLANET SIZES

MERCURY
VENUS
EARTH
MARS
JUPITER
SATURN
URANUS
NEPTUNE
PLUTO

trining the Moon and Jupiter, so the winged messenger within is delivering clear signals, and spreading the news freely and fluently.

Many astrologers like to point out that with Jupiter positioned at 5 degrees of Scorpio, this point as well as any fixed planets or sensitive points at 5 degrees of Leo, Taurus and Aquarius will be particularly affected. But since Jupiter is such a fat planet, I'm not very surgical with this orb, and feel that anything within ten degrees of these points will be impacted. Where Jupiter is transiting your chart—the house it's in and the aspects it's making should shed bright light on what growth is being triggered for you right now. Solar Sagittarians and Pisceans or those with either of these signs as their Rising, Moon, Jupiter, personal planet or prominent point may be influenced more since Jupiter is the ruling planet. The sign and house position Jupiter occupies in your natal chart as well as where it is currently moving represents the most fortunate part of your life. The comet last passed Jupiter on July 7 of 1992, when it came so close that it burst apart into fragments. So perhaps what is being triggered in your life now is an amplification of a cycle which began two years ago when the comet came unglued.

Perhaps the most significant astrological phenomenon is that all eyes are now on the sky and specifically on Jupiter. This mass meditational focus of consciousness on the *great benefic* is both a good sign and a preview of coming attractions. It was God's 21-comet salute signaling the shift into the uplifted Sagittarian period. For by December of 1994, Jupiter will exit Scorpio after a brief conjunction with Pluto, and enter its home fire sign for a year, bound to provide a boost on many levels. A month later, Pluto will leave Scorpio—though just for a 3 month tease—and enter Sagitarrius; so with Pluto & Jupiter in Sagitarrius the vibrational energy should accelerate in these fire signs, like a jet taxiing down the Aquarian runway preparing for takeoff.

While I see the impact as a positive push in our personal lives, it may have some converse or adverse effects on the collective level where power is concentrated. Since Jupiter rules wealth and is very connected to the financial markets, there very well may be some oscillations and disturbances in currency markets, interest rates, and certain investment vehicles. Stay on the sidelines in a defensive and conservative position while financial matters stabilize. Watch for continued shakeups in politics and unusual jolts in the news. This has been accelerating as the comet's have been swarming into Jupiter's magnetosphere or aura in the last month or so. And dare I say, for earthquake prone areas, the window of vulerability is once again certainly ajar. In fact, I suggest hanging out with people you really care about and doing things you truly love during comet week....just in case! But I think it will be a great week.

THE SIGNATURE OF THE COMET

As the comets hurtle toward Jupiter matters in our lives are intensifying. As they have been entering Jupiter's magnetosphere, they have become involved in our auras. Have there been some new developments in your life during the comet's approach? As they make their impacts, the shock waves should ripple through our internal ethers, stimulating positive shifts on the inner planes. It is even possible that a mass awakening or shift will occur from a chain reaction

Edmond Halley

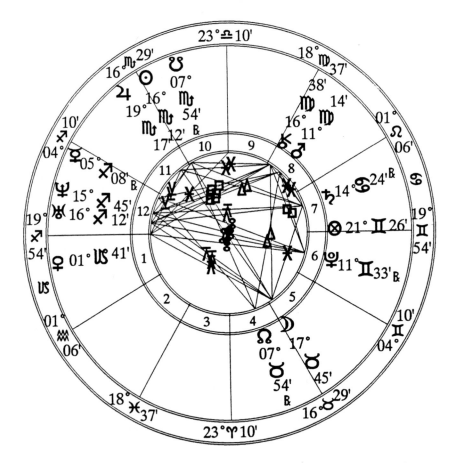

November 8, 1650
10:14:31 AM
London, England

producing a contact high within the universal consciousness. Since this is an unusual and cataclysmic event, I would think there would be some new and striking events happening here in our lives. Perhaps the jolts will be just enough to jump-start the engines of change and get them roaring again in our lives. It certainly feels like a signature event in the universe marking an acceleration of the tremendous shifts in consciousness mankind is making at this incredible time in Earth history.

So go out into the gorgeous summer night sky and gaze up at shining father Jupiter glowing brilliantly in space. Consider how of all the vast places in these deep reaches this comet is coming here. Get ready to experience the biggest explosion man has ever witnessed in our solar system. And as you meditate on the spectacular magnificence of the wonders of creation, please remember how miraculous and good it is just to be alive.

COMET TRAILS: A PRELIMINARY POSCRIPT

The first reports and analysis of the impacts by scientists were even more spectacular than anticipated, with some big surprises. The blast of *fragment G* blazed brighter than Jupiter itself briefly as it blinded telescopes. Several impacts created Earth-size scars releasing energy in the 600,000,000+ tons of TNT range. The lack of hydrogen found in spectographic analysis, along with a preponderance of metallic materials have many astronomer's thinking that this may not have been a comet train at all, *but a series of asteroids!* I can't wait until NASA releases their slide set of photographs, and scientists divulge their digested findings and new revelations about Jupiter, comets, and life.

Earth changes were very prominent during comet week. Four hurricanes swirled in the Pacific, and the longest duration earthquake of the century rolled through Japan lasting 2 1/2 minutes and covering a huge area from Tokyo to the island of Hokaido. There was also a series of eruptions of the Krakatoa volcano, terrible droughts in Puerto Rico, floods in China, a 7.3 earthquake in Vanuatu, a 6.5 off Bali, and huge wildfires in the Pacific Northwest and the Peruvian Andes, among much other heightened activity. It is too soon to determine if these were directly related to the comet crash, but it certainly was a far more active week than usual.

Currency markets were indeed affected as the U.S. dollar sunk to its *all time low* against the Japanese yen.

On the personal level, most people I have talked with had a markedly positive week. For the most part, the reports are of significant leaps in personal growth. The comets or asteroids will continue to rain small debris through the summer to diminish and finish about the time Jupiter enters its zodiacal home, the mutable cosmic fire sign Sagittarius where it will travel through all of 1995. And that's when the real personal growth should begin.

⋆ 15 ⋆

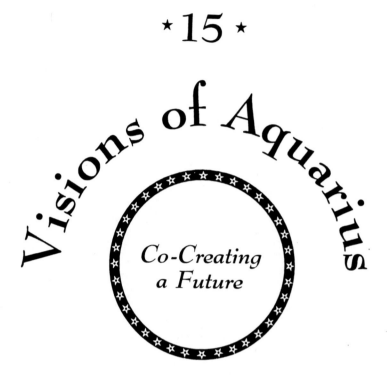

Visions of Aquarius

Co-Creating
a Future

I n January of 1996, Uranus will move into Aquarius, the
sign and age it rules. Welcomed by the transit of Jupiter
through Sagittarius during 1995, as well as Pluto's
entrance into this fire sign, I believe this time demarcates the
shift into the actual commencement point of the true
Aquarian period. But first we must pass through the final eye
of the Piscean needle.

It is always darkest and coldest right before dawn. I do not
expect the Piscean age to die an entirely peaceful death. It is
hard to imagine Pluto finishing out Scorpio, or Uranus and
Neptune completing Capricorn without more upheaval,
destruction, and cataclysm. In fact, the Piscean age will
probably die like a fish wriggling on the line before the
fisherman finally reels him in and puts him out of his misery.

The absolute tragedy the O.J. Simpson situation represents with all of its implications, will pollute and proliferate the mass consciousness for the remainder of the Piscean period. It is itself a negative-polarity Scorpionic reflection of sex, drugs, money, betrayal, violence, distrust, death, and disaster. Not just O.J., but the criminal justice system, the relationship between wealth and justice, peace and justice, race relations, the condition of our society, the role of the media, our psychological obsessions, and the constitution of the United States, are all on trial—in full global view. Big monsters lurk in that swamp. Just one of the many rites of passage during the last few degrees of Pluto in Scorpio, Saturn in Pisces, and Uranus in Capricorn. At this culmination point of the Piscean period, we will take ourselves to the outer threshold of our demise. I'm expecting CNN to rename itself the *Crisis News Network* any day now.

THE AQUARIAN TRANSFORMATION

Uranian energy operates at its fullest potential in its domicile sign of Aquarius. Pluto in Sagittarius promises a spiritual regeneration and a higher direction for manifesting the eternal truths of the universe in our daily lives. Jupiter should prepare, uplift, and light the way in 1995 bouncing through its home sign, Sagittarius. In 1997 Jupiter will conjoin Uranus in Aquarius, expanding and amplifying the magnificent and miraculous potential of the human spirit to its greatest heights. Of course there are also negative manifestations of contrasting Aquarian polarities, and we'll explore these scenarios as well. But the Aquarian period certainly has the incredible potential for a turnaround in the current direction of mankind toward one of heightened consiousness, universal brotherhood, and enlightened humanitarianism. And possibly, even the very survival of our species which spares our civilization and planet, which has rapidly been crumbling like Rome before the Fall. Things will improve and deteriorate rapidly and simultaneously during this powerful transition period.

Heralding this New Age is simultaneously both wonderful and suspicious. This particular period has been declared upon us almost as many times as Chicken Little claimed the sky was falling. The play *Hair*, tried to chanticleer the dawning of this age of Aquarius with the astrological evidence "when the moon is in the 7th house and Jupiter aligns with Mars," supposedly around 1970. For non-astrologers, it is worthy to mention that the moon goes through the seventh house every single day, and Jupiter aligns with Mars at least once every two years. What the heck was *Hair's* astrologer smoking, anyway? To be sure the Uranus/Pluto conjunction of the sixties was synchronous with a powerful global awakening and transformation whose shockwave is still resonating and reverberating. But it was only one of many waves of consciousness we've ridden preparing the way for this period. Another dilution came from the new age movement of the 1980's and early 90's. Though many of the components were very beautiful and beneficial, other accoutrements were rather spurious: Reliance on information from certain sensationalist and greedy trance channels, charlatan gurus, even spacey space beings; an over indulgence in divinatory sources such as tarot cards or psychics for guidance; or giving away personal power to pendulums, synchroenergizers, crystals, and assorted

Aquarian Age

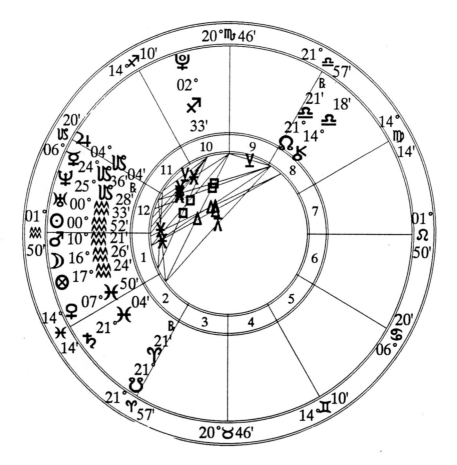

January 21, 1996
7:11 AM
Santa Barbara, CA

miracle cures. But just as the entire planet is going through an accelerated cleansing process at the dawn of another age, new ager's are separating the wheat from the chaff in their gardens as well. Self realization and actualization of one's life purpose to live at full potential is all that should remain.

CUSPS AND AGES 101

By the precession of the equinoxes, ages move backward through the zodiac. Before the Piscean period from which we are emerging, there was the Arien Age, the time of the Roman empire. Before that the Taurean age, then the Geminian, the Cancerian, the Leoneon, and so forth. It takes 26,000 years to complete this entire precession through the ages, with each lasting about 2160 years, though they vary in length. When an age changes its sign, it moves from the first degree of the preceding sign to the last or 30th degree of the new sign it's entering. So we are emerging from the first degree of Pisces into the last degree of Aquarius, with each degree lasting about 70 years. Many astrologers refer to this period as the *cusp*, which both shadows the qualities of the sign and degree from which we are emerging, and foreshadows those of the degree and sign we are entering. Dane Rudyhar's interpretation of the Sabian Symbols for these two degrees illuminates some of the qualities of this cuspal period:

1 **Pisces** - *In a crowded marketplace farmers and middlemen display a great variety of products.* The activity of **Commerce**.

30 **Aquarius** - *Deeply rooted in the past of a very ancient culture, a spiritual brotherhood in which many individual minds*

are merged into the glowing light of a unanimous consciousness is revealed to one who has emerged successfully from his metamorphosis. The state of **Conscious totality of being**.

I feel that the first and last degrees of any sign are usually its most powerful. The first because beginnings are always potent, exhibiting the initiatory thrust necessary to launch the new cycle. The last because the sign has completed its manifestation and expression through the entire cycle of all of its degrees, and is making its final refined and synthesized statement. Cusps are true vortices of intense energy. And with this particular cusp transpiring at both the close of a century *and* a millenium, under our current planetary conditions, is it any wonder we are in a *Grand Catharsis*.

URANUS, THE PLANET

From the moment Uranus was discovered there was upheaval in the traditions of both astronomy and astrology, because Saturn had previously been considered to be the boundary between the solar system and the rest of the universe. Suddenly, there was more to this solar system than met the eye. It is the only planet to be named after a Greek rather than Roman god because the Romans identified the Greek god Chronos with Saturn, who was the son of Uranus, the oldest god. Uranus, which means *heaven*, is the 7th planet from the Sun, located right around the halfway point between the Sun and Pluto. It can barely be seen even with a telescope, so it wasn't discovered until 1781, synchronous with the revolutions in America and abroad. It spins sideways in relation to the rest of the planets, and most of its 15

Abraham Lincoln

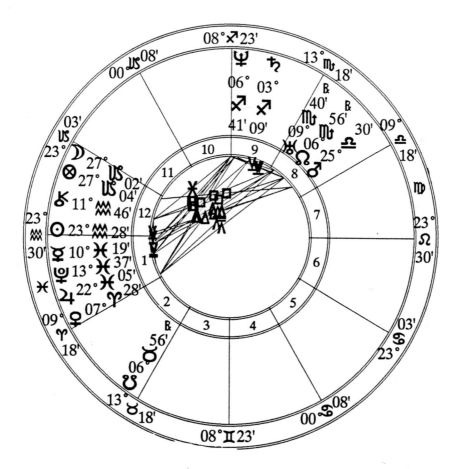

February 12, 1809
12:41 PM
Hodgenville, KY

moons spin retrograde, contrary to all other planetary and satellite motions. It has 11 thin rings, some of which are kept intact by shepherd moons. A blue-green colored gas giant which appears to roll sideways through its 84 year orbit around the sun, Uranus spends 42 years with each of its poles alternately in sunlight and darkness. It is certainly the nonconformist eccentric of our solar system.

URANUS, RULER OF AQUARIUS

In mythology, Uranus was Prometheus, a Greek superbeing who stole fire from the heavens and gave it to humanity. Personified by Aquarian inventor Thomas Edison harnessing electricity into the light bulb: The "man of 90 percent perspiration and 10 % inspiration," also invented the storage battery and the phonograph among his 1000 patented inventions to assist humanity. Uranus rules electricity, science, technology, invention, genius, earth changes, magic, and astrology. The converse of Saturnian structure, it rules the future, the spontaneous, the sudden, the bizarre, the unpredictable, even the wild and manic world of the eternal now. Brilliance, the new & unusual, the cutting edge, the revolutionary, the mad scientist in his laboratory; Uranus is a bit ahead of its time. A rap session between Jonathan Winters and Robin Williams, Christopher Lloyd creating time travel in *Back to the Future*, the journeys of the Lawnmower man; now we're getting Uranian. The ruler of the fixed air sign Aquarius, it is the sign of the magician, the genius, *and* the outlaw; a thin line of morality dividing their dispositions. Thrills, sudden changes, lightning bolts of inspiration; Uranus is the Awakener who breaks the mold then follows the flow. While Saturn is bound by rules, laws, plans, and structures, Uranus is the revolutionary, like Robin Hood, violating them at times in dedication to most humble and humanitarian causes.

There were certainly fireworks the last time Uranus came home to Aquarius between November of 1912 and April of 1919. In those seven years, a nutshell of the more prominent historical events includes the Chinese revolution, World War I, The dissolution of the Middle Eastern Ottoman Empire, The Russian and Bolshevik Revolutions, the formation of the Soviet Union, the Latin American Revolutions, the establisment of modern Israel, and liberation movements in many European Colonies. This was all against the backdrop of Pluto in security conscious Cancer; a period of furious and radical revolutionary change all over this planet. This is also when Japan and the United States emerged as world powers, and when aviation technology reallly *took off*, rising from primitive machines to transcontinenal flight and the first airlines during these seven Uranus in Aquarius years, when evolution accelerates.

AQUARIAN MAGIC

Aquarius has specific rule over the ethers and as we enter this age, the closer we merge with this realm, a heirarchy above our own. This is the domain where the angels live, and the Aquarian period is one where the angel within will be self realized, and where many will merge with the etheric light of higher consciousness along with its enhanced wisdom, knowledge, sensitivity and vision. This higher vibrational field is also where the etheric bodies of many master souls like the

Robin Williams

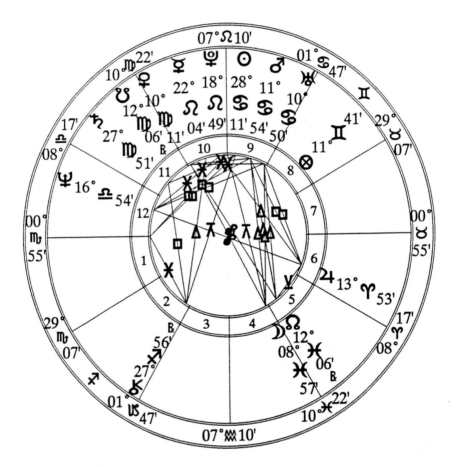

July 21, 1951
1:34 PM
Chicago, Illinois

219

Buddha or Jesus reside, so rising into unity with this domain is how the so-called *Second Coming* is truly realized, or whatever name one wishes to call the state; evolved bliss consciousness, nirvana, samadhi, christ consciousness, or universal love.

In Aquarius we see the symphonic union of art, music, science, & spirituality, as well as humanitarian statesmanship and revolutionary reform. Presidents Franklin Roosevelt & Abraham Lincoln, scientists Emmanuel Swedenborg & Charles Darwin, reformers Thomas Paine & Charles Dickens, musicians Mozart & Schubert, and rastaman Bob Marley were all solar Aquarians. So what about Dan Quayle? Who knows, he may just end up surprising us all.

Sometimes Saturn is assigned the co-rulership of Aquarius, depending on one's stage of evolution. Souls still in need of the tutelage and structure of Saturn resist the receptivity and response to Uranus; those with strong ego structures have developed powerful walls insulating them from the friendly and magnificent opal rays of Uranus. The light bulb is screwed in the socket but it's just not plugged into the juice. But the potential for transformation exists in any moment, so in the course of time, all human beings will awaken and mature to proper attunement with Uranus.

You may find a gender inconsistency in references to Aquarius. This is because this sign is the divine hermaphrodite combining male and female, yin and yang, god and goddess, Sun and Moon, water and spirit; portrayed in the interplay of these polarities in effervescent movement by the two wavy lines of its glyph. Aquarius is Diana the water bearer, clothed in the Sun, standing on the Moon, crowned

Jonathan Winters

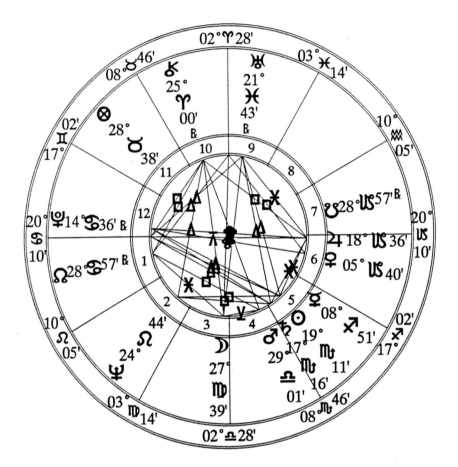

November 11, 1925
8:23 PM
Dayton, Ohio

with the jewels of the twelve star signs, and infused with the wisdom of the keywords, *I know*. In mythology, Aquarius was Ganymede the *cup bearer of the gods*, Zeus' lover who became transformed into the constellation Aquarius. This divine marriage of masculine and feminine natures will help nurture and shepherd the future away from our masculine domineated history into a more balanced direction. Joyously overflowing in its true love for others, Aquarius embraces all humanity through its love and divine compassion for human beings and cosmic kinship with all mankind. As Ralph Waldo Emerson said, "A friend may well be reckoned the masterpiece of nature."

The world is moving into a powerful and magical new force field in this sign and age where all converge into the unity of the christ impulse from our vast diversity where the divinity in every human being glows.

Uranian powered Aquarian energy in its highest evolution is transformative and magical. This sign which synthesizes all of the signs of the zodiac in its etheric incandescence, has the power to transmute the old separative influences of the past to fashion the future while the present still lives. In this union of past, present, and future radiates the positive, creative, corrective magic of love in the eternal now. The world is moving into a powerful and magical new force field in this sign and age where *all* converge into the unity of the christ impulse from our vast diversity where the divinity in every human being glows.

THE ALCHEMICAL INGREDIENTS OF THE AQUARIAN SHIFT IN CONSCIOUSNESS

Way out in the dark abyss of outer space slowly orbits Pluto, the outermost planet of our solar system, representing the deepest, innermost, and most profound power for transformation in human consciousness. Pluto and Uranus are the planets of magic; that power capable of altering space-time reality into a radical shift in the mass consciousness. Pluto has been in Scorpio since 1984 where it dredged the depths & scaled the heights of the human experience, and will now flirt with the cusp of Sagittarius in 1995, before moving in for 15 years in December. The shift from Scorpio to Sagittarius brings forth the myth of the Phoenix, who was reborn into immortality from his own ashes. In *Great Balls of Cosmic Fire* we explored Jupiterian and Sagittarian energy and its fiery, purifying, spiritual, inspirational, benevolent, and joyous upliftment potential. With passionate Pluto now in fiery Sagittarius, a powerful elevation from the bestial depths of Scorpio into the buoyant christ light of divine wisdom will permeate the mass consciousness. Saturn starts building a fresh karmic cycle in the spring of 1996 charging out of the Arien gate. Jovial Jupiter jumps aboard the Aquarian parade in the beginning of 1997, and mystical Neptune joins the Aquarian band in January of 1998. Combined with Uranus in Aquarius, we have the alchemical formula which will create the opportunity for the total transformation of human consciousness to its

Michaelangelo

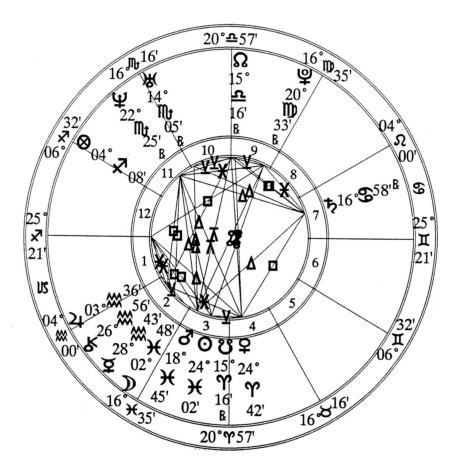

March 15, 1475
1:01 AM
Caprese, Italy

greatest heights, fullest compassion, and finest glory. This movement of the powerful outer planets from water and earth signs to fire and air signs will raise and attune the vibrational frequency of mankind to fertilize the unconscious ground for quantum developmental growth. The universe is conspiring to empower mankind to make a turnaround in its current collision course with catastrophe. But it will be up to each of us to seize this divine opportunity with every fiber of our being in definitive, willfull, and inspired action toward this purpose if we are to be successful. For opportunity means nothing if it is not seized.

Since we have had our feet wet in Pisces so long, it may take a few years to heal up from our Piscean pitfalls and do the Aquarian dance in its full glory. Though most people have envisioned the Aquarian period as one of peace, love, and light, what about all the new Aquarian abnormalities? Afterall, Uranus can also be a pretty zany ruler cooking up some very strange brews for Aquarius to bear in her waters.

Afterall, Uranus can also be a pretty zany ruler cooking up some very strange brews for Aquarius to bear in her waters.

THE TECHNOCRACY OF THE 21st CENTURY

The Aquarian world will be getting more complex and more simple simultaneously. Technology is one area where we will see radical quantum leaps. There is already a dynamic obsolescence of new technologies within the very same year.

Ralph Waldo Emerson

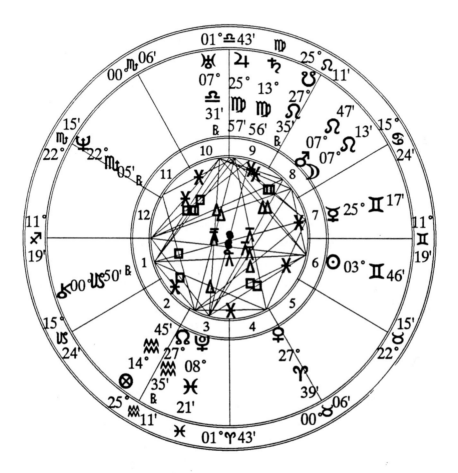

May 25, 1803
7:55:45 PM
Boston, Massachusetts

226

Ten years ago the personal computer seemed somewhat obscure. Now computers of various sorts are an integral part of almost every modern person's life. While today's computers are a hundred times faster than the PC's of ten years ago, the computers of tomorrow will dwarf our current capabilities. The present uses for data management, word processing, or publishing will be integrated with audio, video, telecommunications, television, entertainment, banking, shopping, and investing; making the computer the centerpiece of the average person's life. Even the early Aquarian machines will be smaller, faster, voice activated, and voice responding. A computer akin to Captain Kirk's Star Trek device will appear shortly in the Aquarian future. The personal robot cannot be too far away. Modern man's focus seems to be on making life simpler and easier so he can have more leisure time. The *personal assistant*, who functions as an advanced computer and also does manual skills like cooking and cleaning could soon become standard issue in many Aquarian households. Sort of like your own tame Terminator—perhaps, *the Accomodator*. I even know of some software companies who are working on virtual reality programs for such personal activities as sex. I guess you'll just turn your computer on and get turned on in cyberspace. There is already a wide array of mind-body machines which purport to increase memory and intelligence, stimulate certain desirable brain wave states, and even give you a workout without working out. So how far away can a device which induces total sensorial ecstasy be; kind of like Woody Allen's *Orgasmotron*? Then again, the *Orgasmotron* may take a back seat to simpler methods created by pharmaceutical companies creating new wonder drugs with a similar pleasurable effect; a full medicine chest of new *joy drugs* from the pill fairy.

Will Aquarian mad scientists start tampering with the DNA code to give parents a catalog to create designer babies with just the right color hair and eyes, among other physical and mental attributes. Or will they create a race of 21st century mutant humanoids in their attempts at eliminating our human foibles. Hopefully the Aquarian spirit will direct the innovative genius of its inventions toward more sober, practical and enlightened goals. Cures for a.i.d.s., cancer, and the other horrible blights which manifested in the 20th century should be forthcoming. The merging of Eastern and Western healing modalities should produce many ways and means to retard the aging process and create a veritable fountain of youth. Maybe scientists will even finally find a cure for baldness or the common cold. The Aquarian doctor will integrate nutrition, herbology, stress reduction, exercise, chiropractic, acupuncture, massage and other holistic modalities into his medicine bag. More rejuvenation centers will spring up all over the world. Hopefully even fast food restaurants will fill their menus with healthy foods instead of their current toxic fare, and continue accelerating their environmental concerns and activities.

But where does technology begin invading, polluting, distorting and atrophying the human spirit to the point where it begins to destroy human nature? And what other vulnerabilities does this hyper-technologization create? The more complex things are, the more that can go wrong. Will a society which is so dependent on the computer also be subject to sabotages by genius hackers intent on infecting supercomputers with some doomsday virus? What happens to a country which is trillions and trillions of dollars in debt when its hard drives suddenly crash? Hmmmm. Remember the dreaded *Michaelangelo virus?* What if some triple-aquarian mad scientist succeeds in implanting the *Leonardo da Vinci* or *Robin Hood virus* into the information superhighway or the Federal Reserve, NYSE, VISA, and other computer systems?

One of the laws of machines is that they need periodic maintenance and occasionally break down. The inherent danger of a highly mechanized post modern world so mechanically dependent is if some type of wrench were thrown into the machinery, creating a chain reaction of system breakdowns and an incipient paralysis in the metropolitan areas. This could happen as a result of a cataclysm like a major earthquake, terrorism, war, computer sabotage, or simply system overload: All distinct possibilities in the late 90's. Perhaps if such a breakdown does occur, it will be those more used to living a simple and natural existence who will be the survivors. Will the meek then indeed inherit this Earth?

THE DOUBLE EDGED TECHNOLOGY SWORD

But there will also be a strong backlash to this technocratic trend, with people returning to center on their human attributes and spiritual values. It will take this very saturation in technology to teach people that they don't really need any of it, and that balance is the real key to life.

Aquarian technology will certainly be a double edged sword. Alternative energy vehicles of various sorts will begin to appear with America at the lead, with an estimated one fourth of all vehicles using alternative power by the turn of the

Leonardo Da Vinci

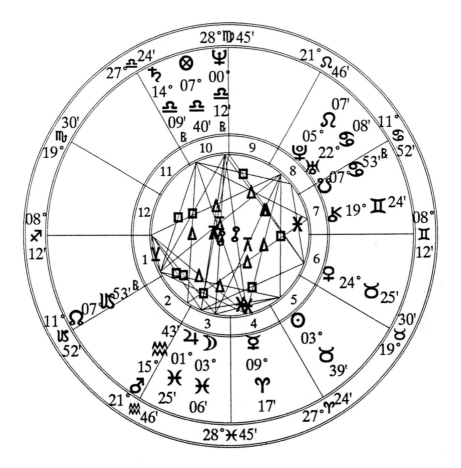

April 14, 1452
09:03:39 PM
Anchiano (Vinci)

230

century! Isn't it interesting that the new environmental requirements of the federal Energy Policy Act go into effect in January of 1996, just as Uranus enters Aquarius. In another few years, it will be hard to find a gasoline powered ground vehicle, with cleaner burning methanol and compressed natural gas taking over. Then again, there may also be sort of a *Mad Max Beyond Thunderdrome* scene going on in some areas as the internal combustion machines become extinct. Clean rapid transit systems will finally connect through our cities. But at the same time, cellular phone companies plan to launch hundreds of space satellites into orbit to create space phone networks accessible from anywhere on the planet. So when you walk out to gaze at your favorite lucky star will you confuse it with something from GTE? I guess that'll be the new way to reach out and touch someone.

THE CREATION OF A FUTURE

Education will be another area where the positive use of technology will be applied. Aquarian classrooms equipped with multimedia computers, cd-roms, electronic encyclopedias, modems, video and other Hitech devices will accelerate adolescent's understanding of human knowledge, and the acquisition and development of skills in foreign languages, business, architecture, medicine, environmental rehabilitation, literature, music, and the arts. Recyling and practical environmental studies must become mandatory courses. If parents can simply assist in guiding their children to keep their spiritual values and priorities in order, there is incredible hope for the future. The shining vibrancy, spiritual radiance, and incredible will to live of the Uranus and Neptune in Sagittarius, Pluto in Scorpio children will blaze a brilliant trail into tomorrow. Many of their parents born during the revolutionary Uranus/Pluto conjunction of the sixties will be wide open to novel directions for themselves and their offspring. Astrology, ruled by Aquarius will flourish and enjoy a new renaissance and be used to assist the understanding and guidance of our children toward a rendezvous with their magnificent destinies. Then if we can simply learn the lesson which our parents have had such difficulty with; to let our children teach us new and better ways of living, we will indeed create a future.

Aquarius rules the 11th house of friends, groups, and organizations and works inclusively in terms of *we* rather than *me*. A major resurgence in alternative community living is taking place where extended families are extricating themselves from the urban pressures of 21st century life, moving to the country and living more self sufficiently by growing food and creating energy from natural sources. Environmentally safe and recyled materials integrated into solar and energy efficient architecturally designed structures will predominate the countryside. Alternative lifestyles filled with health, ritual, music, dance, culture, spiritual values, and lots of love will continue to make more and more sense to more people in the days ahead. Barter systems where goods and services are exchanged in a direct balance with needs will expand. An emerging Aquarian culture who has learned how to live in harmony with each other, with nature, and with God is prepared to flower beautifully into the future, spreading its fertile seeds all over this land.

An emerging Aquarian culture who has learned how to live in harmony with each other, with nature, and with God is prepared to flower beautifully into the future, spreading its fertile seeds all over this land.

And since Aquarius rules friends, the consciousness of the society at large should become friendlier and embrace the inclusive *we* vision as well. As we have seen, catastrophe and cataclysm are the progenitors of true brotherhood, and as we continue to have our disasters, they will bring us back together into the family of man who is also learning that there is really only one true race: the human race. *Good vibrations* will come back into vogue and create a chain reaction of goodwill and feelings. And as Uranus continues into Aquarius and Neptune enters in 1998; cathedrals, shrines, churches, and temples will continue to disintegrate as mankind integrates the knowledge that unconditionally loving God through our pure hearts is the genuine religion where we can *all* join hands. Christ consciousness will be wide awake within those who have tuned in. Prior to this though, alot of dogmatic walls will have to come tumbling down, and it won't be a pretty sight for a while as established religions scramble to keep their flocks from flying. And lots of followers waiting for the personage of a Second Coming may find that it already came, blazing through and irradiating their own hearts and souls. And those waiting for the apocalypse may just miss the boat. There are sure to be massive doses of millenium madness manifesting in a mosiac of wild scenarios akin to the wacko in Wako disaster of 1993, amongst all this weirdness.

And lots of followers waiting for the personage of a Second Coming may find that she already came, blazing through and irradiating their own hearts and souls.

THE FIRST AQUARIAN AGE AMERICAN PRESIDENTIAL ELECTION

This shift into Aquarius is also synchronous with a presidential election. America is truly a Uranian-Aquarian country with both an Aquarian Moon close to the midheaven, and Uranus in a most powerful angular position ascending. Of course, with Uranus, Mars, and the ascendant in Gemini, we are very dualistic in nature; almost like two distinctly different countries in one. Uranus should amplify this polar modality as it moves into Aquarius and awaken the revolutionary spirit. But no matter what reformations transpire internally, I expect the U.S. to be on the cutting edge of lighting the way for all countries into the Aquarian period.

America is truly a Uranian-Aquarian country with both an Aquarian Moon close to the midheaven, and Uranus in a most powerful angular position ascending.

Perhaps with this new Aquarian activitation, Americans will once again be declaring their independence in unique ways. I expect the campaign of 1996 to be the most zany in history. With Aquarius ruling independence, there will be many candidates wanting to run as *independents* besides just Ross Perot and Jerry Brown, with many new *third* parties taking form. Does Scorpio Bob Dole or Aquarian Dan Quayle fit your vision of the enlightened Aquarian leader of the new age? Or will we need to elect a President who is so abominable that he fosters and engenders the revolutionary spirit. I do expect to see the election of 1996 result in a diminution of the power of the Federal government, a greater emphasis on local control, a tax revolt, and a challenge and possible end to the two party system. Perhaps the Clinton's will even step aside leaving the democratic torch to Al Gore who selects a minority woman as his running mate. 1996 is also the year when the new money is scheduled to be put into circulation. Will this transition be harmonious, or will it stir the hot pot of old money issues? Or will the big changes come in the 2000 election when Neptune is in Aquarius and transiting Uranus conjuncts America's Moon?

THE DEVASTATING DOOMSDAY WEAPON: THE POPULATION BOMB

At the beginning of the Piscean age, the entire planet's population was about the same as the United States today; 250 million. It didn't reach a billion until around 1800, and was still under two billion by 1900. Now Earth's population is almost six billion, and projected to double in half a century to twelve billion, with three new people each second! Every new being puts increasing stress every level; physical, psychological, economic, even political.

Now Earth's population is almost six billion, and projected to double in half a century to twelve billion, with three new people on Earth each second!

You don't have to be a quantum mechanic to know that there is already too much stress on our natural resources. I went to a 3 day trade show in Las Vegas recently where I watched 175,000 attendees take home 100 pounds of color printed literature each, to end up in the dump. Flashing that this was just one of hundreds of such events, I started thinking about all the junk mail, newspapers, magazines, packing materials, etc. consumed everyday: I caught another glimpse of the tip of a mammoth trash iceberg which never melts. Which got me thinking about the colossal pressure put on our natural resources everyday. In a recent issue of *Time*, a think tank study found that man has as much impact on the environment every *day* in the 1990's as we had every *year* in the 1940's. And catholic leaders still balk at birth control and abortion! Fortunately almost everyone else agrees that we must reduce the population, and *Earth in the Balance* Vice President Gore will lead a 170 nation summit in Egypt later this year to focus on diffusing the population bomb. He will be freshly armed with the devastation of the horrors in Rwanda demonstrating the long overdue and drastic need for population control. At least we are staring our greatest challenge right between the eyes. But examination without

Bob Marley

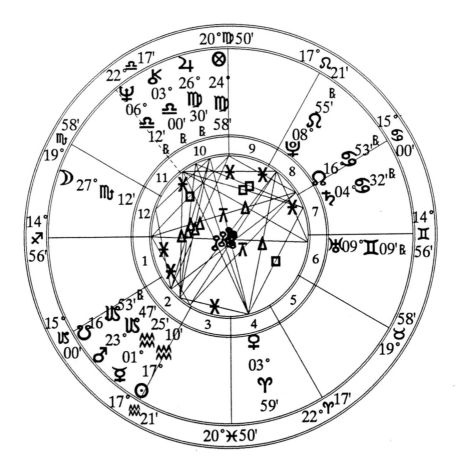

February 6, 1945
2:30 AM
St Ann's Parish, JAM

bold and direct action will no lonfer suffice, so a strict population policy will need to mandated and enforced.

We have taken most of the oil out of this Earth to pollute the air we breathe, while removing the natural lubricant of the Earth's crust. The waste gases from this have heated and distorted the atmosphere and our weather patterns, with most scientists concurring on the reality of global warming and the distinct possibility of a greenhouse effect. We have decimated forests, the lungs of our planet, with nowhere left to put our trash. We have poisoned much of our drinking water, the most precious substance on Earth, polluted our sacred seas, extinguished hundreds of species of life, and with every new being put more stress on the delicate balances of nature. The juxtaposition of watching O.J. spend millions of dollars on his murder defense against the backdrop of millions of his sick, homeless, and dying Rwandan brothers and sisters, is symptomatic of the massive imbalances in the distribution of wealth and resources. It will certainly require some potent Aquarian vision, magic, and medicine, and the activation of brilliant and bold human innovation to reverse these trends for mankind.

Water is the most precious substance on the planet. It is a travesty that in most places we cannot even drink our water, and that it is sold for the same price as gasoline. Keep your personal water supply pure, stay close to water, and if you buy land, make sure you own the water rights. Hopefully the age of the water bearer will empower us with the resources and values to preserve this essence of life.

We cannot continue in the old Piscean pattern where progress is defined solely in economic terms. Wealth must be redefined as the quality of life, not the quantity of money. We must live as a community celebrating life, rather than a commodity exploiting it. Growth must be redefined in terms of renewal—not just as production, consumption, and trade. We must do much more with much less. We must get our money trip *together*.

MONEY AND POWER

Money comes from the word currency whose derivative is *current*. Current is energy, whose basic principle is *flow*. In this pure sense, money is entirely spiritual as it is just like energy and light. The greater and clearer the channels for energy to flow in our lives, the greater our abundance both spiritually and materially. Conversely, when energy is blocked we have scarcity—*Scare-City*. One is love centered the other is fear based. Like the sign Scorpio which rules it, money is very intense, and carries with it alot of emotional charge. The problem with money is another universal principle—balance. If a circuit is overloaded it either trips or burns out. The *if some is good, more is better* philosophy toward the acquisition of money and power on this planet has manifested in such intense greed creating so much imbalance that these universal laws no longer apply. Power without balance destroys the flow and short circuits, or even reverses the polarity of the current. That is when money becomes the *root of all evil*. Everyday we witness outrageous disparities, even tremendous atrocities from this shortcircuited monetary energy. With most people, corporations, and governments engaged in occupying most of their focus, time, and energy in the acquisition of money, there is little wonder we have lost our balance. And for all this energy, the governments of this world are over ten trillion

The Third Millenium

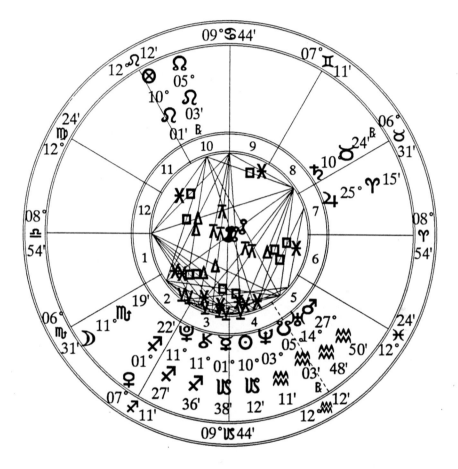

January 1, 2000
12:00 AM
Santa Barbara, CA

dollars in debt! You could not even count to ten trillion in your life if you started right now. And debt has an intrinsic psychological weight to it which sets up an entropic vortex felt by most everyone. Entropic energy can only implode so far before it reverses itself and explodes. The American government, for example spends hundreds of millions of dollars on investigations of non-issues like *Whitewater* instead of housing, feeding, or caring for its citizens or environment. And the citizenry has to foot the bill for this bull. How absurd. The high speed video game of global economics where huge amounts of currency are hedged by governments and bankers while professional traders leverage investments in everything from companies to pork bellies to various types of debt, is both ludicrous and tenuous. Hundreds of billions of dollars are electronically traded in this unbridled and avaricious manner everyday. Until we rebalance and realign our money values with universal law, we are headed toward an economic fall. We had better tame these giant money monsters or they will eat us all alive. Now within our personal lives we *can* live the principles of prosperity and balance, and redefine what true wealth really is; health, functional skills, light, love, happiness, abundance, and fullfillment. And if the power structures and mass consciousness does not awaken to this universal law, in the final Piscean hours, the global economy could easily come tumbling down. Is this what engenders the real meaning of E Plurbus Unum. For it may just take the big economic earthquake for mankind to learn the lessons of money, current, flow, and balance. Remember the Grand Catharsis formula.

It is almost as though there is an evolutionary split going on within the human species. There are those who are

241

aligning with the forces of light and those embracing the darkness; with perhaps a few hybrids as well. This split will continue to diverge as evolution accelerates. Nowhere is this more apparent than when it comes to money. It is critical that the heart and soul and right intention be centered behind livlihood and business dealings. Like Emerson said, "without a rich heart, wealth is an ugly beggar."

But within the Aquarian alchemy there is the magical power of renewal which can bring all things new so that the old is passed away. The same circumstance can seem completely different with a better attitude, so with the amplified vibration of the evolving shifts, the climate for change will improve and transform. Consider how transformed and different you feel before and after a massage, a great workout, some loving sex, or a gut-wrenching belly laugh; somewat analagous to this shift. Just as the human body has the natural will to heal itself, Mother Nature will continue to rebalance herself. Our future as a species depends on our ability to acknowledge, attune, and surrender to these needs, and take radical action to make big changes. So it is up to everyone of us to do *everything* we can right now. After all, good planets *are* hard to find! I am confident that leaders will emerge during this awakened period who will respond by enforcing this vision into statesmanship and a legislative agenda. We must demand and accept no less from anyone representing us. And personally, we have the power to create vital, blessed, healthy, inspired, and attuned lives. So if we do strike out facing our toughest challenges, we'd sure better go down swinging. But I think we're going to make it—by the dangling threads of our collective jimmy-jammies.

Wolfgang Amadeus Mozart

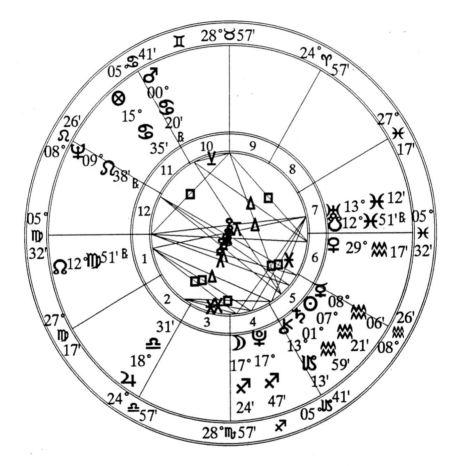

January 27, 1756
7:21 PM
Salzburg, Austria

Our new leaders will face other immediate challenges on the international scene. Has Khadafi forgiven the West for killing his son, has Saddam forgotten about his Jihad. Have these leaders gone back to their drawing boards with ex-Soviet nuclear scientists assisting in the development of renewed arsenals? How solid is the peace between nuclear Israel, Pakistan and the rest of the Arab Middle East? What dwells up the mysterious sleeves of the Chinese and Koreans? Will this planet survive Jupiter's (expansion) conjunction with Uranus in Aquarius while Pluto (nuclear power) blazes in fiery Sagittarius during 1997, without a recalcitrant antichrist-type testing his nuclear power? But if there is a nuclear conflict, it should be much more limited and thoroughly survivable; not the final thermonuclear holocaust showdown which the United States and Soviet Union were heading into during the Cold War. The diminished U.S. and Eastern European threats along with the intense monitoring to enforce nuclear non-proliferation agreements has certainly weakened the former threat of global nuclear annihilation. The other nuclear powers do not have the ICBM's to travel the long distances, though I do worry about Israel. But a strengthening United Nations will be functioning in facilitating a period of world peace. Praise Almighty God, it looks like we have passed the *final conflict* test!

MYSTERIES REVEALED?

What was it that Neil Armstrong saw on his way to the Moon or in the Sea of Tranquility 25 years ago that he's being so coy about? And what exactly are those pyramids all over the face of Mars in the NASA photographs? What really happened in Roswell, New Mexico, and what other information is in the 50,000 or so files the Federal government has on UFO's which they have been refusing to disclose to the public? Are those crop circles which keep cropping up just some college prank? Since we would not even be capable *today* of building the Great Pyramid in Egypt, how was it built in 4000 BC during the Taurean age, and who actually designed and constructed this incredible wonder of the world? And just what information will the recently discovered Dead Sea Scrolls reveal which are under such paranoid protection, and what clues to the identity of Jesus, extraterrestrials, and history will they provide. Many of these questions are also on the cusp of being answered and may help piece together the puzzle of human origins. Within the ripened climate of the higher vibration of Aquarian consciousness, these and other mysteries should be revealed which could also serve to prepare the public consciousness for an ambassadorship with other intelligences, and a new wave of very close encounters with extraterrestrial visitors. What a thrilling time it is to be alive!

THE PROPHETS OF DOOM WERE WRONG

If you had listened to Jeanne Dixon, Edgar Cayce, Criswell, certain Nostradamus scholars, among hundreds of other predictions, this would have already happened in the 1980's. Or if you tuned into Gribbin and Plagemann, Ramtha, Mafu, Ruth Montgomery among scores of others, we would also have suffered the late great Big L.A. Earthquake, pole shifts, among other severe Earth changes. Aquarius should bring clarity in crystallizing the defining point between

Jesus Christ

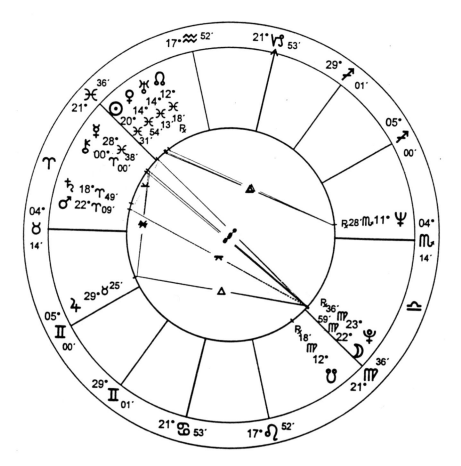

March 13, 0004 BC
6:00 AM
Bethlehem, Israel
(guestimated)

truth and the capitalization on fear? But the problem with psychics has always been their timing, and perhaps their failure to see the entire picture. Psychic images are ruled by dreamy Neptune, ruler of the Piscean age, where astrology is ruled by visionary Aquarius. This is where Nostradamus stood out, because he rendered planetary clues, however obscure, which offered possible time frames of planetary configurations in his quatrains. But what ephemeris was he looking at? And with all those Capricorn/Cancer oppositions and Scorpio Moon, was the brilliant physician and clairvoyant perhaps just a bit on the gloomy doomy side?

This is precisely where the psychics and clairvoyants need the assistance of modern astrology! I have painted a backdrop of the astrological megatrends within which we are operataing, and rendered some clues to stimulate your examination of the future. Furthermore, there will be strong planetary alignments at the end of 1995 and beginning of 1996. A total solar eclipse in 1999 presents a signature of coming changes. And as I've pointed out, there is very powerful astrological and astrophysical evidence suggesting that early May of 2000 could well be the time many of these psychics were envisionining for severe Earth changes. Is this when California, Japan and other vulnerable or overdue areas will make their big break? I don't know for sure, but I'd either be getting very prepared, or moving my rear elsewhere by then. There have been so many warning signs of accelerated seismic activity that anyone who hasn't seen them must truly have their head in the sand. Then again home is where the heart is.

But Earth changes will not only be survivable but will also serve as spiritual catalysts in our catharsis. I have never witnessed more instant activation of true spirituality than during the cataclysms we have already endured. We seem to be at our best when we're up against the ropes. So I expect future catastrophes during this period of Aquarian magic to manifest in grander transformations and greater awakenings of brotherly and sisterly love, and adaptations which bring the human community closer together.

And as I've pointed out, there is very powerful astrological and astrophysical evidence suggesting that early May of 2000 could well be the time many of these psychics were envisionining for severe Earth changes.

The key point is that the changeover will unfold differently and with different timing than any prophecy or prediction has foretold; be it from the speculations of the Bible, the Hopi's, the Aborigines, or any of the clairvoyants, channels, astrologers, gurus, scientists, or arm chair visionaries. Many of their themes are certainly on target, but we are creating our future every moment, and there are some fresh new alchemical ingredients to be added to the brew. Our fate has yet to be written or sealed.

We must awaken to understand and acknowledge what these cataclysms are really all about. Everything in nature is interconnected and in balance except the human ego, and by extension, the massive and terrible violations civilization is impacting on Mother Nature in the name of progress and growth. God and Mother Nature are forgiving. Their balancing forces will eventually redress our present imbalances and restore a new and evolving steady state, with us or without us. But this will involve cataclysm. The task for humanity will be to reverse its destructive trend and implement a vigorous agenda for survival which works with, rather than against nature. The future is thus up to us; God and Mother Nature will certainly do their part. The human race is in the race of its life. But the Aquarian shift gives birth to much greater possibilities for a future.

The human race is in the race of its life.

Another point on which I am crystal clear is that the world will not end in 2000, 2017 or even thereabouts, as many would lead you to believe. An *age* is ending and a *new era* and way of life is beginning. Some of the keys to survival as we move into the 21st century are really very simple: Pay attention and be conscious, stay healthy, centered, flexible, and at peace. Be true to your self, in the presence of those you love, above and away from the madness, and in tune with your higher consciousness which will guide you through your intuition on the right path toward your rendezvous with destiny. Take something you really love to do and master it. Keep your spirits high and create your own heaven in your heart, mind and life. Join hands with your brothers and sisters in transforming your family, your community and this world. In the tough times, dig deeper into your soul for strength from within, which God will provide. Remember that laughter is the healing balm for all catastrophe. An endless fountain of joy, wisdom and timeless beauty is ever present in our hearts and souls. Life and the lifeforce has been blessed upon us to be celebrated. So listen to your heart, follow its sweet song, and live your dreams; the universe will take care of you if you do.

But we must also respond boldly to the challenges of our survival with swift, committed, and radical action. As our consciousness uplifts, so will our creativity and ingenuity in confronting our challenges. If you know of creative lifeways, live them and share them; let love and light fill your life and change our world. The powerful souls who are all here now must focus the brilliance of their hearts and minds to unite powerfully in activating a shared vision of brotherhood on a mission to transform the destiny of mankind. Do not underestimate the magic of the magnificent opal rays of mighty Uranus empowering the sign and age of divine compassion and human innovation. Remember the incredible will to heal and live of all the diverse life forms of Mother Nature. And never doubt the transformative power of love in the universe and the human heart that all will be well: For it is the most vigorous and awesome force of all which *will* engender our Grand Catharsis.

Fortune

Fortunes I've won and lost
Treasures I've lost and gained
But what all has it cost
To me it seems about the same

I've got to taper all my expectations
Down to not a one
And cast them down my desire's throat
And drench them in my Love

Oh hear me lord oh heed me now
In my deepest prayer
Give me all your grace and beauty
Show me that you care

Oh feel me lord and know I am
Becoming one with you
Guide my dreams with your magic
Please make them come true

☆ ☆

Ken Kalb: Thanking His Lucky Stars

The week of January 14, 1994 saw many catastrophes. There were unprecedented firestorms on the eastern coast of Australia. The eastern United States and Canada were chilled by frigid temperatures. Locust swarms threatened to destroy crops in Africa and an epidemic of deadly caterpillars plagued Brazil. More than 10 major earthquakes were recorded worldwide, including the devastating Northridge quake. Can we chalk these events up to plain old coincidence? No, says Ken Kalb, Santa Barbara's astrologer extraordinaire. He thinks these cataclysms are a result of a recent alignment of the planets he dubs a Super Conjunction. And there's more to come.

Kalb, 44, has been interested in astrology since his early teens. A high school math teacher introduced him to the subject when he demonstrated a special knack for geometry. He moved to Santa Barbara in 1966 to attend UCSB. His college years were interspersed with a variety of projects. At one point he owned and operated a holistic health academy on Coast Village Road in Montecito where he gave birth to *low impact aerobics*. A healthy passion for sports and physical activities led him to a stint as a professional tennis player and teacher. His interest in astrology was still strong and he founded the *InnerSpace Institute*, a company he used to publish his astrological writings and research. During his spare time he was able to earn a bachelor's degree in social science. He went on to complete a master's program in health and fitness in 1981.

Around this time he enlarged the focus of the InnerSpace Institute to an astrological chart service. Now known as the Lucky Star Research Institute, he provides astrological charts to thousands of people nationwide. These are nothing like the forecasts found in your daily newspaper. Using a blend of science, intuition, and practical knowledge, Ken develops 15 to 150 page personalized reports for his clients. At each year's end, he sends out questionaires to gauge the accuracy of his profiles. After more than 10 years and 20,000 charts, he has yet to have a client tell him their chart did not fit.

In 1986 he brought the holistic, metaphysical, and creative community together as never before or since in his blockbuster New Age Expo at Earl Warren Showgrounds, attended by thousands of people.

Ken considers himself a practioner of a *New Astrology*. Astrology has been an important part of almost every culture throughout human history. However, modern astrologists have taken advantange of scientific breakthroughs in the understanding of the universe. High speed computer programs which use NASA's data on planetary positions, enable astrologers to pinpoint the exact location of all of the heavenly bodies at the moment and location of a person's birth. Ken uses this raw data plus modern astrological and psychospiritual interpretation to create a chart that fits each individual. Then he uses his intuition and vast astrological knowledge to add his own interpretations and wisdom. He believes he has psychic abilities that aid him in producing accurate readings and forecasts.

As well as using his skills to produce individual charts Ken also gets insights into world politics, upcoming earth changes, and the forward evolution of the human race. His newsletter, *The Lucky Star*, highlights his feelings about the flavor of things to come. The January 1994 issue warned that a planetary *SuperConjunction* on January 11, a time when several planets appear at the same point in the sky, could affect seismic activity throughout the world. One week later we experienced the Northridge earthquake and other major quakes. Ken has also been surprisingly accurate in forecasting other geological activities, political upheavals, and social events.

Ken accounts for his accuracy in two ways. First, thousands of years of astrological data give insight to historical patterns. When an astrological cycle begins to repeat itself, he looks back to historical antecedents to help them predict our present course and future. In other words, if you can accurately predict the past in astrological terms, you should be able to sketch a picture of the future, because "the past, present, and future are all reflected in *the moment.*" Ken also points to scientific studies that show that the movement and positioning of the planets could have major effects on the Earth, because of an inherent *interconnectedness.* When planets align, especially during sunspot peaks, they place a combined gravitational influence on the sun. This has been shown to increase solar activity (such as solar flares, coronal holes, or the solar wind), which in turn interferes with the Earth's atmosphere and magnetic field. As a result, subtle changes in the planet's rotation speed could increase geological activity and might influence other aspects of human life as well.

So what other secrets do the stars hold in our future? Ken feels that the upcoming transition to the Age of Aquarius heralds great changes in our consciousness and way of life. Though he remains optimistic about the outcome of the next few years, he warns that social upheavals, revolutions, and natural catastrophes could be all too common. He urges that people begin now preparing for the *Big One* and work especially hard on developing a deeper sense of compassion for each other and the planet. "We need to treat each other and our planet as sacred, like rare jewels. We must allow the love in our hearts, the creativity of our minds, and the divinity of our spirits create our new world. Even if it takes harrowing cataclysms to shake and wake us up, we need to start making the adaptations and changes to start cooperating and living a lifestyle that will help create a positive future," he said in closing. Whether you believe in astrology or not, a challenge like that might well be worth living up to.

Ken Kalb

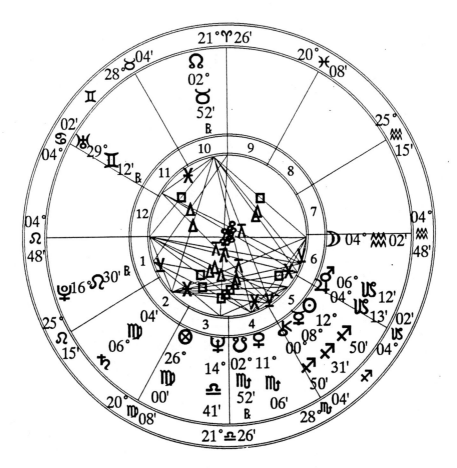

December 4, 1948
8:20 AM
New York City, New York

Astrological Services

Since 1971

Your Lucky Star Profile is prepared combining breakthrough technology in computer programming synthesis, the very latest astrological techniques, and inspired interpretive writing. Your fascinating laser typeset and book-bound narrative features an advanced level of personal analysis - never before possible! Thousands of hours of diligent human effort by our all-star team of top astrologers, writers, programmers, and artists have been devoted to bringing you the finest in astrology. Your report includes a FREE laser chartwheel with an intrepretive key.

BIRTHCHART PROFILE $16.95
An Insightful Personality Profile
Examines your career, talents, health, finances, strengths, & weaknesses, physical/emotional/mental/spiritual makeup: luck, secrets, and much more. Gaze into this astrological mirror to get crystal clear about refining what you're all about. Approximately 15 pages.

THE MASTER LIFE ANALYSIS $29.95
Probing deeply Into Ourselves
The cutting edge: Integrates the most advanced techniques and synthesis to analyze your life through your chart. This 35-page intense astrotherapy session is the most advanced natal interpretation available. Covers similar areas of life as #1, but with greater detail, expoanded perspectives, and wisdom-filled helpful advice.

ASTROFORECAST (Annual) $29.95
Attune Your Life with the Zodiacal Rhythms
We computer precisely date and expertly counsel you on the influences the upcoming planetary movements (`transits') will have as they `aspect' & move through your birthchart. This reliable predictive technique illuminates your upcoming life situation: changes, obstacles, opportunities- & provides graceful wisdom to help you optimize your responses and choices.

PAST LIFE PROFILE $24.95
An Esoteric Look at Your Past Lives & Interlives
Developed after 10 years of meticulous research of thousands of Edgar Cayce readings. Using both Western and Vedic methods, this mind expanding profile looks at the Big Picture of your soul's journey through significant past lives and interlives into the present showing you how to optimize your life *now* & into the *future*! A valuable contribution to metaphysics prepared with the high level of professionalism the greatly respected Edgar Cayce deserves.

ASTROLOGICAL HEALTHSCAN $16.95
A Holistic Health, Diet and Fitness Analysis
This practical report is based on the research of expert medical astrologer Eileen Nauman & supplemented by top health experts. Includes a finely detailed health diagnosis with full spectrum therapies for balancing your biochemistry for optimum health. Hippocrates himself insisted that astrological analysis was fundamental to diagnosis, treatment, and good health.

⑥ ADVANCED NUMEROLOGY REPORT $16.95
A Full Life Reading Based on Pythagorean Numerology
An integrated and probing narrative of your life's path, deepest inner desires, karmic mission, lessons, & debts; soul's urge, optimum environments, relationship qualities, & much more. And now - we analyze both your Birth Name and your Current Name (please include both!) - to describe the changes this creates in your life.

⑦ THE UNIVERSE WITHIN $24.95
Heart and Soul Centered Astrology
With the brilliance, wit, grace, & charm of celebrated astrologer Stephen Forrest, a deep & lyrical narrative of your life is woven into one outstanding 20-page profile. Great for newcomers & oldtimers to astrology alike, you'll get a refreshing new vision of yourself. Even interprets Karmic nodes & Soul Archetypes. You'll love it! FREE. with (#9) THE WORKS!

★ ★ ★ ★ ★ ★ ★ ★ ★ ★ **DISCOUNT PACKAGES** ★ ★ ★ ★ ★ ★ ★ ★ ★ ★ ★

⑧ THE MAXI-COMBO $49.95
A Bargain Package on Our Finest Interpretive & Predictive Reports
Get a Master Life Analysis and an Annual AstroForecast together and save 20%!

⑨ THE WORKS! $99.95
All the Above Individual Reports at a Big Discount Plus Special Bonuses!
Get a Birthchart Profile, A Master Life Analysis, an Annual AstroForecast, A Past Life Profile, An Astrological HealthScan, an Advanced Numerology Report, The Universe Within - plus a laminated Color Birthwheel and special Bonus features. Save BIGTIME!!!!!!!!!!!!!!!!!!

★ ★

⑩ THE COMPATIBILITY REPORT (Non-Romantic) $24.95
Understanding the Dynamics of Your Personal Relationships
A Comprehensive analysis of all of the intricacies and delicacies of any type of relationship - friends, co-workers, associates, relatives, you name it! Uses the most popular synastry techniques - cross aspects, planets in partner's houses, cusp synthesis, and more - to create this fascinating and helpful profile.

⑪ THE LOVE REPORT $29.95
See how the Stars in the Sky match the Stars in Your Eyes
Similar to #6 but also explores sexuality, intimacy, & the other interactions within the lover's domain. Includes an examination of common factors in both natal charts *and* your Composite chart for a complete *Book of your Love.*

⑫ THE CHILD'S PROFILE $24.95
Brilliant Parental Guidance
A fabulous new report for kids - focusing on the developmental inssues during upbringing & how astrology can help optimize it. Potentials & assets, problems & pitfalls, relations with parents; direction, destiny, educational & profression directions, probability of worldly success; nutrition, health, & much more are all detailed. Powerful material for every parent & child!

⑬ RELOCATION SURVEY $24.95
Scout Before you Travel or Move
An accurate & helpful report analyzing your changbes in different locations. Pick 4 places you may considering for moving, travel, business, vacation, or ?: A report will be written for each. ($ 8 for each extra location over 4) Note: Locations in close proximity may only have minor (yet important) differences.

FOR WOMEN ONLY! $29.95
Planets, houses, cusps, signs, and aspects interpreted especially for the female
ecifically designed for women, with a focus on self improvement. Romance & sex, profession,
lth, nutrition, money, your relationship with each sign, past life influences, family matters, &
ch more are illuminated in this special *gender-specific* light. 30 Sensational pages!

SOLAR RETURN FORECAST $24.95
Your Annual Rebirth Year Preview
integrated predictive report painting a vivid picture of the principal changes of your year from
thday to birthday; signifying your annual Rebirth! Specify where you were on your birthday.
n be done for different years and locations. Please specify.

FULL COLOR BIRTHCHART $12
The Most Beautiful Charts in the Solar System
tted in 7 gorgeous colors on an artistic backdrop then progessionally laminated, these
artwheels are an absolute Knockout! Great gifts. FREE with The Works. Just $8 extra when
order any report(s).

THE GRAND CATHARSIS $14.95
An Astrolog of the Shifting Ages
anthology of Ken Kalb's finest published articles, several new articles, 60 charts, poems,
strations, & much more in a 250 page book with a beautiful visionary art color cover.

★ ★ ★ ★ ★ ★ ★ ★ ★ ★ ★ ★ **ORDER FORM** ★ ★ ★ ★ ★ ★ ★ ★ ★ ★ ★ ★

me_____   **Second Person:** (for compatibility or love reports,

dress _____   when ordering for another, or for birth certificate name)

ty/State/Zip _____   Name_____

one_____   Birthdate_____
                                              MONTH   DAY   YEAR
rthdate _____   Birthtime _____
   MONTH   DAY   YEAR

rthtime (if known) _____   Birthplace _____
 birthtime is unknown we will use a solar rectification)   CITY   STATE   COUNTRY

rthplace _____
   CITY   STATE   COUNTRY   *Thank You Very Much!*

★ ★

M #	TYPE OF REPORT	PRICE		Please complete form & send with check to:
				Lucky Star
				Box 5796
				Santa Barbara, CA 93150
				(805) 969-4401 (800)969-4401
	SUB TOTAL			**24 hour instant order line:**
	7.75% TAX (CA ONLY)			**1(800) 626-2721 ext. 405**
				Charges only.
	SHIPPING	$2	50	For credit card orders:
	TOTAL			MasterCard ☐ VISA ☐

Name (on card) _____
Signature _____
Card _____Exp ____